IAS/IPS SUCCESS PATH

IAS/IPS SUCCESS PATH

DR. RANJIT KUMAR SINGH, IAS (AIR-49)

PRABHAT PRAKASHAN

Published by

PRABHAT PRAKASHAN PVT. LTD.
4/19 Asaf Ali Road,
New Delhi-110 002 (INDIA)
e-mail: prabhatbooks@gmail.com

ISBN 978-93-5488-670-6
IAS/IPS SUCCESS PATH
by Dr. Ranjit Kumar Singh, IAS (AIR-49)

Edition
2025

Price
₹ 300 (Rupees Three Hundred Only)

Printed at
SS Japan Arts, Delhi

Author's Note

The Union Public Service Commission conducts an all-India examination annually Civil Services Examination. This examination is held in three stages - Preliminary Examination, Main Examination and Interview. The Preliminary Examination is a screening test, the copy of which is objective and alternative type. While the Main Examination is a written examination in which the depth of study and analytical ability of the applicants is tested. In the final stage of the examination, the personal qualities and contemporary awareness of the candidates are tested through the Interview. The Civil Services are the most prestigious and liable in the country. Out of a population of 150 crores, about one thousand civil servants are selected every year, even though lakhs of candidates apply. The significance of Civil Services can be easily understood from the above figures.

The candidates for these services are tested on a three-tier test. The candidate who fulfils these tests with passion and zeal is selected and takes an oath to serve the country by spreading his unique aura. In this book of mine, the applicants of the Civil Services are introduced to certain habits to help them prepare for the examination. The applicants could easily qualify for the UPSC exam if they implement these certain habits in their daily life.

I am sure you all must be wondering, from where did I get the inspiration to write this book? It is the story of those days when I used to study in the sixth grade. While going back and forth from school, I would come across a bookstall. At the bookstall, I would search for books related to topics such as 'What Are the

Qualifications Required to Become an IAS Officer,' 'When and How Can One Appear in the Civil Services Examination,' etc.

There hardly went a day when I have not searched books related to the title "How to Become an IAS Officer." But I always met with disappointment. Frequently I would give 20-30 rupees as advance to the bookseller so that he could get such books for me from anywhere. But this discovery of mine continued even after passing the 10th board exam. Even after becoming an IAS officer, I did not find a book which would meet my expectations.

As I am penning this book, my childhood memories are coming back. Hopefully, this book will successfully fulfil the quest of the curious minds of all UPSC aspirants. I wish everyone a bright future.

❑

Contents

1

Civil Services Examination: An Excellent Way to Prepare

When any educated youth thinks about his career, he gives the utmost importance to three factors – position, prestige, and job security. All these three requirements can be fulfilled in only one career and that is the civil services. The Indian Civil Services is the most prestigious service in the country, which has always attracted ambitious, capable youth who accept challenges. From this point of view, the civil services is the only career that establishes a balance between both personal ambition and social responsibility. That is the reason why lakhs of youths in the country try their luck to join the civil services as compared to employment-oriented fields like medicine, engineering, and management.

At the beginning of his or her career, a civil servant gets the opportunity to work in many important and responsible positions which is not so in other career fields. The wide range of work is the specialty of this sector.

If you are dedicated and serious about the IAS/IPS exam, then it is important to know the best way to prepare for them. To be aware how difficult an exam is, one should look at its success average. Based on this criterion, the IAS/IPS exam can be said to be the toughest exam. Its success average is 0.01 percent. To crack such exams, mere commitment, preparation, and luck are not enough. For this, it is necessary that the candidate should make regular preparation for his or her lifestyle. At first, it may seem most cumbersome. But if you are dedicated and serious about the exam, then there can be no better way to prepare for it than by making exam preparation a part of your lifestyle.

If you want to succeed in the exam, then one need not tell you how imperative it is to make a timetable for your studies. Your timetable should balance study hours, rest, physical activity, and social life. Studying constantly will lead to monotony and you will lose interest in your studies. So, make two or three different time schedules, wherein the daily, weekly, and monthly goals of your studies are fixed. This will enable you to monitor your preparation and make corrections where necessary.

The syllabus of the UPSC exam is really vast and covers the entire range of subjects. In this scenario, many candidates try to memorize the facts instead of understanding the concepts. This method is absolutely wrong. Our memory can store only a limited amount of data and it also fades with time. So, it is very important that you understand the basic concept of whatever you read. If you understand a subject well, then you will be able to remember all the information related to it satisfactorily.

Many candidates focus only on the preliminary examination, which has objective-type questions. Initially, this strategy may sound right, but later you will realize that it is wrong. The mains exam of IAS/IPS is a traditional subjective type exam in which you have to write answers manually by hand. So, if you want to crack the mains as well, then it would be advisable that you start honing your writing skills from the prelims level itself. Many experts are of the opinion that studying accompanied by writing is not only one of the best ways to remember factual information, but it also helps in developing the format of answers, which proves advantageous in the main examination.

Newspapers are the best friends of an IAS/IPS aspirant. So, you should make a habit of reading newspapers daily. However, this is not enough. You should also identify the topics on which you need to focus more. Before starting to read newspapers, ask yourself what you should read, why you should read, and where you should read it from. In this way, you will read only what is relevant and continue to collect new necessary updated information every day.

What most candidates fail to notice is that government websites are a simple and accessible source of policies, plans, programmes, data, and reports. The information that you get and the understanding that you will develop by studying these websites will be beneficial in both the prelims and main examinations.

IAS/IPS aspirants should continue to have healthy and high-quality discussions with their fellow aspirants, teachers and coaching instructors. During these discussions, focus on one topic, look at it from different points of view, and take your point forward on the basis of authentic data. You will be able to write more balanced and complete answers in the examination when you are exposed to different points of view on a topic. Being a member of such discussion groups motivates one to study and also helps in preparing for the interview.

You will need problem-solving skills not only to crack the exam but also while working as an officer later. You will come across many challenges, which you will have to handle, with the help of new techniques. You may have to deal with the challenges of studying the vast syllabus, time management, resources, peer pressure, societal pressure, etc. In such situations, your problem-solving attitude will come in handy.

Preparing for the IAS/IPS is a long and exhausting task. The syllabus seems to continuously expand and time seems to continuously shrink. In such a situation, depending on one teacher, guide, mentor, or coaching class material does not help. You have to become your own teacher. Formulate your own questions and find answers using references and study materials. Playing the roles of both teacher and student will also instil confidence in you, which will be useful during the exam and beyond.

The policy of 'only work, and no play' cannot work in the preparation for the IAS/IPS examination. To date, no one has cleared the IAS/IPS examination by locking himself/herself in a room with many books. You should also pay attention to your health, entertainment, and social life. Take out time every day for yoga, meditation, running or sports, etc. Eat nutritious food and get at least eight hours of sleep daily. Spend time with family and make friends who share your goals and objectives. This will keep you focused and motivated.

The journey to success in the examination is very long and difficult. Only your commitment will help you in completing this journey. You will come across many such challenges and difficulties, which can make you feel uncertain. There are many young people who, after spending five to seven years in the preparation for the exam, give up owing to societal pressure or continuous failure. Despite such challenges, it is also true that every year a handful of candidates crack this exam through sheer will power. For this, it is necessary that you have faith in yourself and dedication towards your goal.

Besides, due to the increasing competition, it is becoming difficult for candidates to crack the IAS/IPS exam. One of the main reasons that make this exam so difficult is that apart from your knowledge, it also tests your lifestyle, your personality, and your character traits. Knowledge can be obtained from books and resources, but we cannot get information about lifestyle qualities such as self-discipline, motivation, punctuality, and other facts from books.

These are part of individual lifestyles and develop over time. Such qualities mark a significant difference between the candidates when it comes to the final selection.

You must have heard from your teachers, coaches, and even classmates that the key to attempting the IAS/IPS exam is studying. They are not misleading you. The only way to get through the ever-expanding syllabus of the CSAT exam and even the extensive syllabi of subject-specific papers is to develop the habit of self-study. This habit of studying cannot be forced on you, it should come naturally to you. So, if you are preparing for the Civil Services Examination then being a bookworm and voracious reader will definitely help you. Apart from gaining knowledge with the help of books, you can also learn by improving your language skills and writing style.

History of Civil Services Examinations in India

The British made a huge contribution to in the administrative structure of India that we see today. The Union Public Service Commission is also one of them. The history of the Civil Services in India is much older than the history of New India and has long been one of the strongest pillars of the country's progress.

Lord Cornwallis is considered to be the 'Father of Civil Services' in India. He started and organized these services in the eighteenth century for the smooth running of the administration. For many years there was no examination for an appointment to these services. But the revolution of 1857 forced the British to change the system of administration. After 1857, the Parliament of England took over the governance of India. After a few years, the Indian Civil Service Act of 1861 was passed and some posts were reserved for contractual civil servants (who had lived in India for at least seven years).

This opened the doors to the highest ranks of the civil service for Indians. An arrangement was made that for recruitment to the administrative services, an entrance examination in English medium would be held in England, which would have subjects like Greek and Latin languages, etc. Initially, the prescribed age for this exam was 23 years. Thereafter, it was reduced to 22 years in 1860, then to 21 years in 1866, and finally to 19 years in 1878. Indians were also allowed to appear for this examination. However, on account of many hindrances, it was difficult for Indians to take this exam. There were several reasons for this, such as the examination was held only in England and its syllabus was also beyond the understanding of Indians. The curriculum emphasized the knowledge of Greek, Latin and English languages. Despite all these limitations, in 1863, Satyendranath Tagore (Rabindranath Tagore's elder brother) achieved the distinction of being the first Indian to succeed in the Indian Civil Service. Given the work profile and rights involved in this post, in 1885, Congress in its first session demanded the Indianization of 'Public Service'.

After this, Lord Dufferin set up the Aitchison Committee (1886) to recommend changes in the civil service. The committee proposed that the contractual and non-contractual civil services be renamed as Imperial, Provincial, and Subordinate Civil Services, respectively. Gradually the ICS came to be known as the "Steel Frame" of British control in India as it provided essential support to the British Empire in maintaining control over vast territories. Then in 1917, with the August Proclamation by Edwin Montague in the House of Commons, which promised to increase the involvement of Indians in administration, the percentage of Indians in public service began to rise significantly. Then after a few years in 1923, the Viscount Lee Commission was established. This commission was created with the aim of improving public services. The major recommendations made by the commission were-

(i) The process of appointments to Indian Civil Service, Indian Police, Indian Medical Service, Indian Engineering Service (Engineers of Irrigation Department), and Indian Forest Service, etc. should continue and the appointment should be made by the Secretary of State for India.

(ii) Any further appointment or recruitment to other services at the All-India level, such as the Indian Agricultural Service, the Indian Veterinary Service, the Indian Educational Service, the Indian Engineering Service (Roads and Buildings Branch), and the Indian Forest Service (in

Bombay Province only) should not be made. In the future, the appointment and control of the members of these services should be under the provincial governments.

(iii) For the Indianization of services, 20 per cent of the higher posts should be filled on the basis of promotion from the Provincial Civil Services.

At the time of direct recruitment, the ratio of British and Indians should be equal so that the ratio of 50-50 could be achieved in about 15 years.

(iv) Retirement should be allowed on a proportionate pension basis to such British officers who were not willing to serve under Indian ministers.

(v) The 'Public Service Commission' should be set up as per the provisions of the Government of India Act, 1919.

Accepting the above five recommendations of the Lee Commission, the British Government implemented them and established the 'Central Public Service Commission' in 1926 and entrusted the commission with the task of recruiting public servants. There was a provision for a chairman and four other members in this commission. Its first chairman was Sir Ross Barker, a senior member of the British Home Civil Service. When the Governance Act of 1935 came into force, the name of this commission was changed to 'Federal Public Service Commission'. When the Constitution of Independent India was implemented on January 26, 1950, then the name of the 'Federal Public Service Commission' was changed to 'Union Public Service Commission'. In Hindi, it is called *'Sangh Lok Seva Ayog'* and in English, it is called the Union Public Service Commission.

The UPSC is responsible for conducting the Civil Services Examination to select and recommend candidates for Civil Services appointments. The exam is based on the model used by the Imperial Civil Service for years.

In 1976, a three-stage selection process was recommended by the Kothari Committee. The preliminary examination is objective in nature, consisting of one paper each for optional and general studies. The main examination consists of nine subjective papers. The personality test is the last stage. In 1989, the Satish Chandra Committee suggested including an essay paper and improvement of interview (personality test) marks. In 2004, the commission proposed that a qualifying certificate be included in the preliminary examination. Then in 2011, CSAT was added to the preliminary exam and in 2015, it was made qualifying.

What is UPSC Civil Services Exam?

The UPSC conducts Civil Services Examination every year, which is also known as the 'IAS/IPS Exam'. UPSC conducts around a dozen exams for various services like engineering, medical, forest service, etc.

UPSC is an independent organization for the recruitment of Level A and Level B employees. The Union Public Service Commission (UPSC) was established on October 1, 1926. It is headquartered in New Delhi. UPSC conducts civil services competitive examination every year in the country. On the basis of its results, civil service officers like district magistrates, IPS/police officers, etc. are selected for central and state administration of the Government of India.

Required Educational Qualification

According to UPSC, candidates applying for the exam must be graduates in any stream. People with postgraduate and higher education can also apply. If you have a professional degree equivalent to it, you are still eligible to apply. If you have studied at a foreign university, you can get information regarding this by visiting the official website of the UPSC.

Age Limit and Number of Attempts

Considering the age limit for the IAS/IPS exam, it has been set differently for different categories. According to the commission, the age limit for general category candidates is from 21 to 32 years. OBC category candidates are given a relaxation of 3 years, while SC and ST category candidates are given a relaxation of 5 years. General category candidates can appear for the exam 6 times. The OBC category candidates can appear for this exam 9 times and SC-ST candidates can attempt it till the maximum age.

Selection Process

First, the preliminary examination is conducted. All the candidates who have applied can appear for this exam. Candidates who clear the preliminary exam get a chance to appear in the main exam. Candidates who pass the main exam are called for an interview. A merit list of those who pass all these three exams is prepared on the basis of their scores, and their rank is determined. Those who score a good rank get into the IAS, while the rest get into services like the IPS, IFS, and IRS.

Preliminary Examination

In this examination, two papers have to be attempted, which are conducted on the same day. The first paper is General Studies and the second paper is Civil Services Aptitude Test. Each paper carries 200 marks and all questions are objective type. Two hours are given to solve each question paper. One important aspect related to this exam is that the aggregate of preliminary exam marks is not added to the final exam, but without clearing the preliminary exam, you cannot appear for the main exam. The preliminary examination is an important stage to filter the candidates for the Main Examination.

Main Examination

After clearing the preliminary examination, one can appear for the main examination. There are a total of nine papers and all of them are subjective types. The first two papers in this exam are of qualifying nature, which only have to be passed and their marks are not added to the final merit list. Altogether in the nine papers, there are about 180 to 200 questions, and the total marks are 1750.

The time allotted for each paper is three hours. Paper A is not compulsory for candidates from the states of Arunachal Pradesh, Manipur, Meghalaya, Mizoram, Nagaland, and Sikkim as well as for hearing-impaired candidates.

Interview

This is the last stage of the exam which carries 750 marks. This is the most important phase of the Civil Services Examination. Candidates are called to Delhi to participate in this phase, where a fixed panel asks them questions.

Only the marks obtained in the main examination and interview are added to the final merit list.

Cut-off

It is very difficult to predict the cut-off of any exam, but a trend can be traced by looking at the results of previous years. For example, the cut-off in the preliminary exam is usually around 50 percent, in the main exam it is 35-40 percent and the final merit list is also prepared on a 45 percent cut-off.

Eligibility for UPSC examination

The UPSC is the central agency of India, which conducts the examinations like Civil Services Examination to recruit candidates for many top government services like IAS, IPS, and IFS, or we can say that it is the agency responsible for the examination of Group A and B employees of the Indian and Central Services. The commission is accountable to the President of India. Since the UPSC is a constitutional body, it functions entirely under the provisions of the constitution. Although the constitution gives everyone the right to join the government and its institutions, the same constitution also allows those institutions to set certain eligibility criteria according to their needs.

The eligibility for the UPSC exam is the first consideration to be taken care of by the candidates. So candidates must keep an eye on any change in eligibility criteria through the official website of UPSC. Some of the basic eligibility criteria are based on factors like nationality, age limit, educational qualification, and number of attempts –

Nationality

If you are planning to appear for the UPSC (IAS or IPS) exam, you must be a citizen of India to be eligible to apply. For other services, the candidate must be-

1. Citizen of India or
2. Citizen of Nepal or
3. Citizen of Bhutan or
4. Those Tibetan refugees who came to India before January 1, 1962, with the intention of settling in India or
5. Persons of Indian Origin (PIOs) who have fled from Pakistan, Burma, Sri Lanka, and East African countries like Kenya, Uganda, United Republic of Tanzania (Tanzania, Zambia, Malawi, Ethiopia, Zaire, and Vietnam) to permanently settle in India.

Note: *Candidates belonging to Category 2-5 should produce a certificate of eligibility issued by the Government of India. Before obtaining the said eligibility certificate, they will have to appear for the examination and they will receive the offer of appointment only after the certificate is issued.*

Persons belonging to Category 2–4 are not eligible for appointment to the Indian Foreign Service.

Age Limit

The minimum age of a candidate for the UPSC (IAS/IPS) should not be less than 21 years and not more than 32 years as on the date fixed in the advertisement.

The table below shows the age limit for each category of applicants –

Category	Age (Exemption)	Number of Attempts Permitted
General/EWS	32	06
OBC	35 (relaxation of 3 years)	09
SC/ST	37 (relaxation of 5 years)	Unlimited (Up to age limit)
Defence Services Personnel	35 (relaxation of 3 years)	09
Persons with benchmark disabilities (PWD)	42 (relaxation of 10 years)	Unlimited (Up to age limit)

Number of Attempts

A maximum of six attempts are allowed for a general category candidate in the UPSC (IAS/IPS) Civil Services Examination. However, the restriction on the number of attempts is not applicable for SC/ST category candidates. OBC and candidates with benchmark disabilities are allowed a maximum of nine attempts at the exam. The number of attempts becomes an important factor in applying for the Civil Services Examination.

If a candidate appears for any one paper of the Preliminary Examination, he/she is deemed to have made one attempt at the Civil Services Examination.

Candidates who are appointed to the Indian Administrative Services or the Indian Foreign Services and continue to be members of that service are not eligible to appear for the IAS exam again. They have to resign in order to compete again in the Civil Services Examination. A serving IPS officer can appear for the Civil Services Examination again, but they cannot opt for the police service.

Educational Qualification

The minimum educational criteria for the UPSC (IAS/IPS) exam are as follows –

1. Candidates must possess a degree or equivalent qualification from a university recognized by the government.
2. Those candidates who are in the final year of their higher education course or waiting for the result are also eligible to appear for the preliminary exam. For the main examination, along with the application, they will have to submit proof of having passed the said examination.
3. Candidates with professional and technical qualifications recognized by the Government as equivalent to a professional and technical degree are also eligible.
4. Medical students who have passed the final year of their MBBS degree but have not completed their internship are also eligible for the exam. They will have to submit the course completion certificate (including internship) from the concerned authority of the University/Institute.

Success Story: Self-Confidence and Positive Attitude

There are many UPSC aspirants who, despite achieving success, keep striving for a high rank. Most of these people achieve success. One such IAS officer is - Priyank Kishor, who got an All-India Rank 61 in the UPSC 2019 exam and became an IAS officer.

Priyank had got success in the UPSC on the first attempt, but his rank was 274. According to that, he was selected for the Indian Accounts and Audit Service although his dream was to become an IAS officer. So, he decided to try again. On the second attempt, he scored a good rank and according to his wish, he got the post of IAS officer. In this way, he joined the list of such candidates, who cleared the UPSC exam twice in a row.

Confidence and a Positive Attitude are Essential

Priyank believes that it is very important to have self-confidence and a positive attitude to get success in the UPSC exam. If you prepare with a positive attitude, you will be able to perform better. Apart from this, self-confidence is also an important aspect to gain success. According to him, the UPSC prelims exam should be taken very seriously because if you get stuck here, your journey will be over.

Find Shortcomings and Fix Them

Priyank got 274th rank in the UPSC 2018. In this situation, he did not lose his confidence and decided that he could improve his rank by rectifying his shortcomings. He identified the shortcomings of his first attempt and tried to correct them. Apart from that, he practised his answer writing skills and appeared for the second attempt with an all-out effort. His hard work and diligence paid off and on the second attempt, he got the post in the IAS as per his wish.

How to understand the scientific aspect of IAS/IPS preparation

Friends, UPSC preparation is an enjoyable journey in itself and only he can enjoy this journey who prepares for it by immersing himself completely in it. Although there is no guarantee of success and failure one thing is certain that success in this exam cannot be achieved without proper analysis. If someone has analysed this exam properly, that is, has understood the science of this exam, then his journey definitely becomes easier than other students. Let us know and be aware of what the scientific approach to clear the UPSC is.

How do we prepare for the UPSC? What should one read, and what should one not read? Which topics need special attention or from which topics are the questions framed and how? These are some of the questions that often bother students. But the chances of the students to be successful increase who prepare for this exam with a scientific approach.

When we understand every aspect of a situation, know its rules, and then make our preparations based on those rules, it is called the scientific approach. Now you might wonder as to how the scientific approach can be applied to UPSC as its subjects are mainly related to humanity. But friends, you can also apply a scientific approach to the subjects of humanity. Believe me, once you start doing so, you will not only be able to understand these topics easily but also not need to memorize facts.

For example, take Polity. While studying politics, if we keep in mind how those topics are related to our life or society and try to understand their relation, then we will understand that topic easily and remember it for a long time. Suppose you are reading about fundamental rights. While reading about them, try to understand how a right affects a person and a society or try to understand what our society would be like in the absence of that fundamental right.

Similarly, let us look at history. While reading history, we should always try to relate it to the present. While reading, try to understand what could have been the reasons behind any change in the society of that time to society today. For example, when we read Vedic history, we learn that at that time women had a very respectable position and status, but gradually there was a decline in their status. By the end of the medieval era, their condition had become quite pathetic. Thus, while reading, focus on the reasons that could be responsible for this change.

If we talk about geography, then this subject is already considered quite scientific. If you try to understand the facts conceptually instead of rote learning, you will realize that this subject is very simple. Along with this, the possibility of making a mistake in it will also be negligible.

Environment is one subject in the UPSC that troubles many students because you cannot find any reliable book for it. But if you combine geography with current events, you can easily prepare for this subject.

The UPSC syllabus may seem scattered. But when you study it in depth, you will realize that it also has some rules, on the basis of which questions are prepared. When you understand those rules, it will become easy for you to prepare even those topics that are considered difficult.

Which is the most difficult stage of the IAS/IPS exam- The preliminary exam, the main exam, or the interview?

The UPSC Civil Services Exam is considered one of the toughest exams not only in the country but also in the whole world. Actually, the syllabus of this exam is so extensive and the pattern is so rigorous that it is considered to be the second most demanding exam in the world. You already know that the UPSC exam is conducted in three phases. But let us know about the most difficult phase among these.

People consider it the toughest exam for different reasons. It is difficult for some people because the percentage of success in it is very low. Some consider it the most difficult exam owing to the vastness and extensiveness of its subject, while there are others who find it difficult due to its pattern.

As far as its different stages are concerned, each person grades them differently according to difficulty in their opinion. In such a situation, it would be appropriate to talk about all three phases separately so that you can get a complete understanding about each phase.

The first stage of the examination is the preliminary examination. It is an objective type of test with a maximum of 100 questions to be answered in 2 hours. This stage is considered difficult because of its multiple-choice pattern. Often, doubts arise in the mind when one looks at the options and the answer turns out to be wrong. At the same time, the pressure of answering as many questions correctly in less time also makes the candidates commit mistakes. Apart from this, as it is the first stage, the competition is also very high (out of about 10 lakh people, only 15,000 people are able to clear this stage.)

The second stage is the main examination. Most people consider this stage as the most difficult one because here one has to write the answers and almost every question is asked to know your opinion on an issue. That means in this stage, you have to express your view, which sounds very easy but is equally difficult to explain. Apart from this, there are examinations of many subjects in this phase which lasts for seven days. This pattern is quite exhausting for the candidates. It is difficult to maintain the energy till the end. Apart from this, at this stage, there is competition among serious candidates, and out of 15000 people, only 2500-3000 people succeed.

The third stage is the interview which is very tough as there is no fixed syllabus. The interview panel can ask you questions on any issue and you don't even know what impact your answer has on them. As far as the competition at this stage is concerned, it is the toughest among all the three stages. This is because 2500-3000 intellectually superior people, selected from a crowd of one million people, compete among themselves for less than 1000 seats.

Thus, it is certainly difficult to decide which stage is the toughest among all the three stages of the IAS/IPS exam. But one thing is certain - when these three stages are combined, then the exam definitely becomes the toughest.

UPSC: Preparation for Preliminary and Mains-Together or Separately

There are many dilemmas in the minds of the candidates preparing for the IAS/IPS. The biggest dilemma among these is whether the preparation for preliminary and mains should be carried out together or separately. In fact, the UPSC syllabus is so immense that aspirants and especially those who are just starting their preparation do not understand which stage they should prepare for first and which later.

Different people have different views as to the stage from which the IAS/IPS preparation should be started. Some people advise preparing for the mains first, while others advise preparing for the preliminary exam first. The supporters of both sides also have their own arguments. But if you go through the complete IAS/IPS syllabus properly, one can understand that the preparation for both these phases should be carried out together.

Actually, there is not much difference between the syllabus of the preliminary examination and the main examination. So, while studying you can complete both syllabi simultaneously. But since the patterns of both exams are completely different from each other, one needs to be careful while studying.

As you know, the preliminary exam paper contains objective-type questions. In this, you are given a question with four options, out of which you have to choose the correct option. Two marks are awarded for every correct answer and 0.33 marks are deducted for every wrong answer. This rule of negative marking makes this exam even more difficult. The objective of this stage of examination is to weed out the non-serious candidates from the competition. Apart from this, the purpose of this test is also to assess the reading and comprehension ability of the candidates. Your information, understanding, and accuracy are tested at the preliminary level. The answer to each question is right in front of you; all you have to do is find it and mark it within the given time.

Similarly, the objective of the main exam is to test your point of view and your knowledge. Apart from this, this phase also tests your ability to put your knowledge on paper. Overall, your knowledge, writing and presentation skills are tested in this exam.

Now as far as preparing for both stages is concerned, you can carry out self-study for both stages simultaneously as the syllabus is the same. Start with the basics, then continue studying to gradually increase your knowledge. While reading, focus on every word and try to develop your own point of view on each issue. In this way, you can gain knowledge and information together to prepare for both phases.

But there is a vast difference between both phases and that is clearly visible in the answer-writing practice. But you can prepare for them together; if you want, you can prepare for different stages on different days of the week.

However, as soon as the date of the prelims approaches, you should concentrate on the prelims exam only and set aside the answer-writing practice of the mains exam. Essentially, no matter how much you study for the preliminary exam, its pattern is such that if mock preparation is not done, then the exam will certainly be difficult.

Subjects Studied in UPSC (IAS/IPS) Preparation

The IAS/IPS is called India's toughest exam for a reason. The syllabus of the exam is so vast that it requires a lot of time and focus to crack it. Those preparing for the IAS/IPS believe that any questions under the sun could be asked in the exam. That is to say, you have to be knowledgeable about many different areas while preparing for the exam. Questions can be asked from any field in the exam. For example, under general knowledge and current affairs, questions are asked from every area and you have to prepare accordingly.

Even though it is vast, the IAS/IPS exam also has its own prescribed syllabus, under which there is a list of subjects to be studied and the topics included in them, and the questions of the exam are also asked from within these subjects. So, let us know and be aware about the subjects from which questions are asked in the UPSC.

General Science

This subject mainly includes both general science and general knowledge. In this, questions are asked from all the fields of science. That's why it should be studied thoroughly and meticulously from the beginning. This is a very important subject because questions from many areas are covered in it. In this, there are general questions from physics, chemistry, biology, and other subjects of science as well as mathematics.

History of India and the Indian National Movement-

History is one of the main subjects of the UPSC. In this, you have to read about the history of India and also the major movements in the history of India. The history of our country is very vast and interesting. There are many such incidents or rather movements in history, without which it is not possible to understand today's India. In this subject, you read about how movements have played a key role in the history of India, when and who carried out the movements, their purpose, and many more things about the history of India. Questions are also asked about how the history of India has changed over time, the roles played by various people, etc. You should prepare for this subject with the help of the best books.

Current Events of National and International Importance

Current affairs are also a part of the main subjects of UPSC. If you want to pass the UPSC exam, then you need to have accurate knowledge about the current events in every field. You should be aware of all the important current events not only in our country but also in foreign countries. Along with the written test, this subject also plays a pivotal role in the interview. All such recent events, which are of national or international importance, come under current topics. In order to have complete knowledge of current events, you should regularly read newspapers and magazines specially designed for this.

Geography of India and the World

Along with history, the geography of India and the world is also one of the major subjects of the UPSC, in which you are asked questions related to the geographical structure of India as well as the geography of India, such as - how many rivers are there in India, which river passes through which state, etc. Questions are asked about the rain forests of India, topography, etc. Along with this, questions related to the weather, climate, etc. of India also come under geography.

Questions related to sustainable development, poverty, inclusion, demography, initiatives taken in the social sector, etc. also come under geography. Under this subject, the economic condition and economy of the country are also studied. Topics such as how social development is taking place in the country and how it should occur, what is sustainable development, how sustainable development can be done, etc. are also to be read within this subject.

Indian Polity and Governance - Constitution, Political System, Panchayati Raj, Official Issues, Public Policy

Since the UPSC exam consists of topics related to Administrative Services, i.e., Indian Constitution and Social Justice and Law, for this exam, you have to study about Indian Polity, Indian Constitution, Social Justice, and International Law and Relations. It is also important to know which law in the constitution of the country is meant for which kind of work so that you have accurate knowledge of the constitution and law of the country and as an officer, you can follow these rules properly and as required.

General Issues Related to Environmental Ecology, Biodiversity, and Climate Change

This is also an important subject in the IAS/IPS exam under which questions are asked about the different types of animals and trees found in our country, i.e., biodiversity of our country. Under this subject, you are taught about the natural disasters that occur in the country and about the prevention and security management of those disasters.

IAS/IPS Exam and Mental Health

Lakhs of students try their luck in this exam. Some of them find success, while others learn a lesson and prepare again the next year. In the midst of the pressure of the examination, most of the students leave the failure behind and try to move forward, while there are some students who go into depression and even take extreme steps like suicide.

If you have decided to become IAS/IPS, welcome to this biggest and toughest battle of the country, with also a prayer to God for you to sustain your patience, confidence, and enthusiasm for a long time because these aspects are absolutely necessary.

Students need to take care of their mental health while preparing for exams. Almost all the students have negative thoughts in their minds, and sometimes it becomes difficult for the students to handle them. You can follow these steps to maintain your mental health –

For their studies, students should draw up a schedule (timetable) that helps their bodies and minds to function optimally. While studying, you should take a break of a few minutes in between and refresh yourself and resume studying again. Also, sleep at the right time every day because adequate sleep is very important.

Most students spend a lot of time studying, which results in minimal physical activity. Due to this, the body becomes lethargic and there are negative thoughts in the mind. That's why along with studying, it is necessary to spend one hour for exercise.

Yoga and meditation also help the students to concentrate on their studies, have mental peace, strength, and reduce negativity. If you acquire the ability to control your mind and brain through 15 minutes of yoga every day, it will greatly benefit you in your studies. Create a group in which everyone motivates each other. Regular exercise is necessary to focus on studies during examinations.

Students can also take the help of technology. There are many apps available that help in developing health, such as proper sleep routines, better eating habits, etc. Consume milk, seasonal fruits, and vegetables, almonds, walnuts, raisins, sprouts, etc., and drink plenty of water. Keep up your confidence and feel happy and blessed that by the grace of God, you have got the opportunity to study, learn, face exams, prove yourself, and achieve success.

During the preparation for the exam, frequently, students get worried about their performance and results. To avoid this, do not take too much pressure, rather get involved in things like music and art. This will keep you positive. Parents of such students should also not put extra pressure on them regarding studies because nowadays children know what they need to do for superlative performance and career.

The quality of mental strength works not only in IAS/IPS preparation but also in every walk of life. It is much needed, or you can say it is mandatory where the target is big and difficult, and obviously, the aim to become an IAS/IPS officer is a herculean and difficult target.

Benefits of Preparing for the IAS/IPS Exam

Every year around ten lakh people try their luck in the UPSC Civil Services Examination. Or we can say that some of them test their perseverance and personality with this criterion. However, even among these few, there are only a handful who succeed in the examination. But have you ever thought about what happens to those who prepare sincerely but are unable to succeed due to some reason? Is there no way left for them to move forward in life? Are they left empty-handed after dedicating the crucial years of their life to preparation?

In order to become an IAS/IPS officer, one has to work hard, read numerous books, and deeply understand a number of topics. If after putting in so much hard work and devoting so much time you don't succeed, then all the deligence is of no use. If you want to start the preparation again, you have to start again from zero, and if you leave the preparation and opt for another job. Even if you want to give up the preparation and try for some other job, you have to start from scratch. After hearing all this, you may feel that if you do not qualify for the UPSC, you will not get any benefit from it in the future. But this is not entirely true. If you prepare for the UPSC with full sincerity and dedication, then you definitely gain some things which give you an advantage in other competitions in life. Some of them are as follows –

Confidence

During the preparation for IAS/IPS, you study a lot, which increases your knowledge, and with the increase in knowledge, confidence automatically comes.

Your Performance in Normal Life

While preparing for the exam, you learn many new things related to your life. This improves your performance in normal life as well.

Responsible Citizen

When you read about your rights, duties, rules, acts, etc., you try to follow them because after getting the position, an IAS officer has to make these policies.

Knowledge of All Fields

It is well known that the syllabus of the IAS/IPS is very vast. So, you have to study many topics from different fields. As a result, you can freely express your views on any issue or have a good group discussion on the related issue.

Performance in Other Fields

After preparing for the IAS/IPS, unfortunately even if you don't get selected, you can perform better than normal people by doing things in a different way wherever you are working.

Other Ventures

Apart from this, you gain so much knowledge that you can make a career as a journalist, writer, teacher (guide), social worker, or in any field.

For the almost 15-20 years, another situation is being seen in the case of competitive examinations, i.e., on the lines of IAS, each state conducts its own civil service examinations. Through this, the Deputy Collector, Deputy Superintendent of Police, and other officers are appointed. One remarkable thing that is observed is that 80 to 85 percent of the successful students in these services of the state are those who had prepared for the IAS/IPS exam earlier, i.e., they are actually preparing for the IAS/IPS, but they also appear for state examinations. If they are not successful there, they become successful here. Basically, UPSC is a very comprehensive exam, which includes the preparation of many other competitive exams. All that is required is that you dedicate yourself to this comprehensive syllabus to the best of your ability. You must have heard the saying –

No effort ever fails.

Even if the goal is not achieved, the distance will diminish.

To which destination does this diminishing distance take you? If you search for the answer, you will eventually come to the conclusion that 'my IAS preparation will not go in vain, if I don't let it go in vain'.

❑

2

The Process of Exam Preparation

There is always a certain curiosity among students about the 'Civil Services Examination', one of the topmost examinations in the country. The present young generation is quite apprehensive about their employment and career. In today's time, every young person in society wants to get the best job so that he can spend his life happily and contentedly with his family. That's why today's youth works hard hard to make a career in the field of the civil service.

The attraction that was there towards the ICS services during the British era has not diminished even today. The civil service is the backbone of the Indian administrative system. The formulation of policies in the country and their implementation is mainly the responsibility of civil servants. This is the reason why the importance and social identity of civil servants has become prominent, especially in a developing country like India.

First Step to IAS/IPS Preparation

Even a journey of a thousand miles begins with a single step. Often, we get scared even before moving forward and retreat upon seeing the difficulties along the way. But victory ultimately belongs to those who consider their destination to be more important than the path and keep their efforts focused.

The IAS/IPS exam is not difficult, rather aspirants' intentions are weak. Firstly, not everyone is serious about the IAS/IPS preparation. They are overcome by the feeling that since others are doing it, they should do it, too. If you are also preparing for IAS/IPS for the same reason, then you should give up now and make a career in your desired field. But if you are really serious about the IAS/IPS, then discard all the fear and take your first step towards the UPSC.

If you want to reach the top, you have to start climbing. But keep in mind that climbing to the top is not an easy task because as you go higher, the climb becomes increasingly difficult. You have to mould yourself as a dignified personality and as a civil service student, you have to move forward to fulfil this mission of becoming an IAS/IPS officer.

Fear prevents you from doing many things in life. It is the fear that stops you from even dreaming about civil services. It is the fear that keeps many people from even thinking of attempting the IAS/IPS exam. Remember, fear is only a state of mind that can be overcome by perfect preparation and skilful practice. Prepare for the IAS/IPS exam with courage and enthusiasm and also keep examining and practising for your personal growth. Keep in mind that the key to your success in the IAS/IPS interview is your dignified personality and balanced thinking.

Will power is such a magic potion that can take you to any height of success. Stick to your determination to become an IAS/IPS and do not harbour any confusion or doubt. For the development of knowledge, you also require to get help from other sources. Therefore, keep seeking guidance and directions from your seniors and experts.

Having control over yourself is the basic step towards self-improvement. You are the master of your life, so it is not right to blame circumstances or others for your failures, these are just excuses. If the son of a rickshaw puller, a waiter in a restaurant, blind women, physically challenged people, or people who perpetually underperform in elementary school or college can fulfil the dream of becoming an IAS officer, so can you.

No success is possible without hard work and dedication. To be successful, you have to step out of your comfort zone and take the necessary steps in your own interest. Instead of complaining about what you do not have, always be thankful to God for what you have now. If you are fit in your mind and body, you will definitely be able to clear this exam. All you need is the right attitude and confidence. So, always be positive and uncompromising.

Time lost can never be regained. So, do not waste it on futile activities. Improve your productivity by learning time management techniques in order to prepare for the IAS exam. When it comes to being successful in life, a disciplined routine is very important and only a disciplined aspirant can crack the IAS exam.

With whom is the real competition in the UPSC exam preparation?

You have made up your mind to prepare for the civil services, you have collected all the information for it, and you are also preparing diligently. But have you ever thought about who your real competitor is in this exam? No? Then let me tell you.

There is a very popular notion about the IAS/IPS exam. Only those who make themselves eligible for it can achieve this goal. It is not important whether he is preparing with the help of any coaching class or on his own. The point is whether he is fit to be a civil servant or not. Now you must wonder how to know whether you are eligible for the IAS/IPS or not. So, for this, you should observe some qualities of the qualifying candidates and if possible, observe the candidates who live in villages. If you have noticed, a large number of candidates appearing for the exam come from a rural background. They are often unknown faces in the crowd as they prepare and when the results appear, everyone realizes that this person was in our midst all these days and we never saw them!

Actually, life in the village is so full of difficulties that the students there often develop such abilities which the students living in the city are not able to do. Perhaps this is the reason why the number of students who qualify for the IAS/IPS is more from the villages of Bihar and Uttar Pradesh.

It seems that the Civil Services Examination has been deliberately designed for failure. Most of the candidates, many of whom clear the exam, also fail multiple times in one or more stages of the three-stage exam. Strong faith and the ability to persevere in the face of temporary setbacks help them and eventually they are successful. There is a need to keep preparing by having faith in yourself. The village students are more determined in this matter. They are not afraid of failure, rather they keep moving forward by making failure their ladder.

The most important quality of a serious Civil Services aspirant is the ability to do hard work with dedication.

The Civil Services Exam is among such exams which even students from many premier institutes of the country often fail to crack. Only a good academic record and high intelligence can take you far in this exam and of course, there is hardly any substitute for hard work. On the other hand, candidates from relatively unknown colleges and 'modest' educational backgrounds often crack the exam. Exams prove the truth that 'hard work can beat talent when talent doesn't work hard'.

How should new candidates prepare for the IAS/IPS?

The IAS exam is different from other exams in many ways. Its syllabus and pattern are such that even good students cannot find a way out of its whirlpool. But there are some students who understand the nature of this exam, prepare for it and achieve success. To be successful in this exam, it is very important that its preparation should be started as early as possible. But from where should the preparation start or what should be the preparation strategy? It is also very imperative to understand this.

Before starting the preparation, you must gather some important information. What is the Civil Services Exam, what is the eligibility for it and what is its syllabus? After the basics are clear, you can make a good strategy. There is a difference between the preparations for the UPSC preliminary and main exams. For the preliminary exam, you will need a lot of information but not in-depth, whereas, for the main exam, you will need to have in-depth knowledge of the subjects.

Make a Timetable

To become an IAS/IPS officer, it is necessary to be like an officer with a well-organized daily routine. You should set a comfortable timetable before you start your preparation and work accordingly. Making a timetable will make your preparation easier and more organized, you will do better work and also complete the syllabus faster.

Choosing the right books

Choosing the right books is also necessary for preparation. You should study those books which are recommended for the **CS** exam. You should read those books twice. In the first instance, read all the chapters one by one. In the second instance, read only the important chapters. It will be advisable if you go through these books once again before the preliminary exam or main exam.

Read NCERT Books

The National Council of Educational Research and Training (NCERT) is an independent agency with a mission to provide high-quality education to Indian school children. A variety of study materials is available for the IAS/IPS exam. But it is recommended to start with NCERT books that discuss the concepts in simple terms. Students are advised to read NCERT books from Class VI to XII for relevant subjects. However, since NCERT alone will not take you far, you must ensure that these books are covered as soon as possible. It would be best to finish them during the first three months of your preparation.

You must read newspapers

If you want to become an IAS/IPS officer, then you must know that reading newspapers is essential for the IAS/IPS preparation. Keep yourself informed about what is happening in the world. Current affairs are really dynamic topics, about which one can learn by reading newspapers.

Make a schedule and stick to it

When you start preparations at home, there is a chance that you will become lethargic. So, you should plan the schedule for 10-12 months for this. Divide your time between Paper 1 and Paper 2. Paper 2 in the preliminary examination is only of a qualifying nature. So, don't focus too much on that. Instead, you should focus more on Paper 1, i.e., General Studies.

Assess your preparation

You must take mock tests frequently. With this, you will know in which direction your preparation is going. Accordingly, you will be able to change your strategy.

Revision

When you prepare for a tough exam like the IAS/IPS, revision becomes essential. Since the syllabus is vast and varied and covers a wide range of topics, it is not easy to recall things that you have studied earlier. To avoid this, it is very necessary to revise the material periodically.

The most important aspect of this journey for IAS/IPS is to remain positive. There are moments when the atmosphere can be very tense and you may feel anxious or nervous. You must remove all negative thoughts from your mind and heart and just keep focused on your work.

At what age should you start IAS/IPS preparation?

There are many aspirants who wonder what the right age and time to start preparing for Civil Services (IAS/IPS) Exam are. Although the UPSC has fixed the minimum age of 21 years to appear for the exam, the IAS has not set any age limit as to when to start preparing.

Although there is no specific age to start preparing for the IAS/IPS most of the candidates start preparing for this exam just after graduation at the age of 21 or 22. But there are many candidates who try to join the civil services even later and start preparing at the age of 26 or 28. We have also come across candidates who appeared for the exam at the age of 31 and cracked it on their very first attempt. You cannot prepare for civil services in 3-4 days. For this, you have to spend a lot of time studying and this preparation may also take about two or three years. Your determination is very important. Therefore, it is very important for the students to know the appropriate age to start preparing for the exam so that they can achieve success with minimal attempts.

Some students decide to prepare for the Civil Services Examination from the age of 18 itself. Eighteen years is considered ideal for completing higher secondary studies. After completing higher secondary school, students enter college for graduation. Students pursuing graduation get a golden opportunity to choose subjects for graduation keeping in mind the IAS/IPS exam, which would benefit them while choosing optional subjects for the main exam. If we analyse the statistics of the candidates who have been successful in this exam, we learn that most of the successful candidates started preparing for the exam at the age of 18. After completing graduation in three to four years, students can appear for the UPSC exam at the age of 21 or 22. There is also a possibility that an IAS/IPS aspirant at the age of 21 or 22, after completing graduation, may crack the exam in his first attempt. But it will depend on how seriously he/she has tried to cover the exam syllabus during graduation.

There are also many students who decide to prepare for the IAS/IPS exam after completing their graduation at the age of 21 or 22. A candidate must have at least a Bachelor's degree to be eligible to appear for the exam. After completing graduation, students have adequate time at hand which they can devote to IAS/IPS exam preparation. There are many IAS/IPS toppers who decided to prepare for the exam after completing their graduation at the age of 21 or 22. There are many students who focus their attention on preparing for the exam alongside completing their graduation and enrolling for postgraduation courses.

There is no particular or ideal age to start preparing for the IAS/IPS exam. However, on analysing the success rate of toppers, we can say that an IAS/IPS aspirant should start preparing for the exam at the age of 21 or 22 after completing graduation.

How to prepare for the UPSC (IAS/IPS) preliminary exam while staying at home?

First of all, you should understand the pattern and syllabus of the exam. There is a very common misconception about the UPSC that there is no limit to the questions asked in it. But the truth is that the UPSC has posted information about the syllabus on its website and the questions asked in the exam are within the ambit of this syllabus. You must spend four to five days understanding it and selecting your subjects first. You can also get an idea of what is covered in the syllabus and how it is covered by looking at the topics given in the official syllabus and also old question papers. You can also know about the topics with the help of Google.

The second important step towards cracking the IAS/IPS exam is to draw your preparation roadmap. To understand which subject to study and when and how to study it, you can watch the videos of toppers on YouTube and learn how they prepared their roadmap. Apart from this, there are many blogs by the toppers related to the roadmap available on the internet and you should read them.

Now the next step is to start your studies seriously. First of all, go through the conceptual topics which are from the five main subjects that you have selected. Keep the target of fully finishing the topics therein by November. If possible, simultaneously start preparing yourself for CSAT as well. For this, check your score yourself by solving old question papers. If you manage to score 100 in mock tests at home, believe it or not, you don't need to prepare intensively as only 66 marks are required to qualify.

Many aspirants think that they should read from and consult new sources. But if successful candidates are to be believed, it is more beneficial to prepare from the already available classic sources. Along with this, keep track of how many chapters and pages you read per day. Focus on core topics. Core topics are also good for working professionals. After this, prepare for basic science and technology and current affairs together. Then ethics remains to be studied, which you can study even after the preliminary exam.

For current affairs, you should read daily newspapers and magazines. Read newspapers daily for a maximum of 45 minutes per day, do not spend more time than this. After December, focus completely on the preliminary exam. You should solve previous years' question papers along with studying the syllabus of the preliminary exam. During this time, forget about the main exam and just focus on the preliminary exam. Take one test every week and then finally practise one or two test series per day.

Try to solve previous years' question papers topic-wise. Keep solving the questions from both the preliminary exam and main exam related to the topic you are studying and finally try to revise each topic more than once.

It is not necessary to study for 18 to 20 hours. You can be successful even by studying for 8-10 hours with full and absolute concentration.

Smart Work Vs Hard Work in IAS/IPS

Perseverance is the most important thing to succeed in the exam. With such a vast syllabus and such a different pattern, there is no other option than hard work to succeed in it. But one thing should be noted here which is given that the competition in this exam is so tough the right strategy is also required along with concerted efforts. That means having the right strategy is also essential to make hard work lead to success.

As we discussed earlier, success in the IAS/IPS exam can be achieved only by combining both hard and smart work. Both have their own importance. But the question as to which of these two concepts should be primary often confuses people and to remove this confusion, it is necessary to understand the meaning of these two.

Hard work means working diligently to complete any task and to be successful in that. If a labourer builds a building with full effort, it is his hard work. Similarly, if a student studies diligently, then he is also doing hard work. On the other hand, smart work means working hard using your intellectual ability, which will lead to faster and better results, such as a construction worker using a tool or machine to reduce his physical labour, or a student using someone's notes to make studies easier, or discussing a topic with his friends and understanding it so that there is no need to read it repeatedly.

Let us understand which of these two is more important.

Some Points of Hard Work

Dedication

It is most important for a person to be dedicated to hard work. The path of hard work is long, boring, and tiring, and without dedication, it becomes difficult to stay on the path. But if you are dedicated, then you do not get distracted by any challenge because you have confidence in yourself that you will overcome that challenge.

Experience

One of the advantages of travelling along a long route is that you get many experiences during the journey, which prove to be helpful in the future. Also, they can forewarn you about upcoming challenges.

Painful

The path of hard work is very painful. It is not necessary that this suffering should be only physical. For IAS/IPS aspirants, this process is more at the mental level. There will be times when your heart will want to do something else. But your mind will tell you that studying is most important. At such times, you may often study, but you will not understand anything.

The method of hard work is based on traditions that have been followed for years. But the world is changing rapidly and many traditions are also breaking down or slowly becoming obsolete. For example, there are two ways of taking classes - one, in the classroom i.e., the traditional way, or two, with the help of the internet on a computer or mobile which can be called a modern way. The biggest problem with the traditional method is that it takes considerable and immense effort and reduces efficiency.

The Features of Smart Work

Smart work not only removes the deficiencies of hard work but also strengthens its positive aspects. The biggest advantage of smart work is that it saves your time and you can do more work in the extra time that is left with you. For example, reading a chapter completely and making notes from it is hard work, which you have to do in any case. However, instead of reading the chapter over and over again to remember it, it is smart work to go through those notes again and again. With this, you will be able to recall the entire chapter in less time, and in the time saved, you can study some other topic.

It is impossible to choose between hard work and smart work. It is like choosing between your two hands or two feet. Both have their own importance and success can be guaranteed only by using both together.

Coordination of Timetable and Strategy in IAS/IPS Preparation

Students who start preparing for the IAS/IPS often have many dilemmas. Numerous types of questions keep arising in their minds. This is very natural because when one jumps into this ocean, initially, one does not know which way to go, where to start, and how to proceed.

Most people believe that before starting the preparation for the IAS/IPS exam, one should prepare the exam's blueprint. With this, you can reach your destination in a better way. For this, first of all, you should see your syllabus. After this, you should collect NCERT books from Classes 6 to 12. You should start your preparation with these books alone and should not read any other book till you go through them at least twice.

Follow the syllabus of the exam strictly while studying or you might miss important points in the bid to cover every point. Practise the previous year's questions every day along with the syllabus. Before reading any chapter, try to read the questions of that chapter. With this, you will know which points to pay more attention to while reading the chapter. To study smartly, it is also necessary to keep evaluating your preparation from time to time. When you do this, you will know whether your preparation is progressing in the right direction or not. You can take mock tests to check your preparation. For this, you can also take the help of any online portal or coaching institute. If you do not want to take the help of any coaching institute, you can practise mock tests at home with the help of Prabhat Prakashan's 'Previous Year's Questions' or 'Mock Test Papers'.

Truly speaking, your success depends on how you manage your time. The syllabus of the IAS/IPS exam is so infinite that it takes a lot of time to cover it entirely. So, avoid making unnecessary notes and do not waste time on unnecessary topics. Make optimum use of your time for your studies. For example, you can read newspapers and magazines while having breakfast or before going to bed. In this way, you will not need to allot separate time for studying current affairs.

As you are aware the IAS/IPS exam is conducted in three phases and all three phases are quite distinct from each other. So, the strategy should also be different for the three phases. The preliminary exam has objective-type questions and negative marking is very important in it. Often students are not careful about this aspect and fail at the preliminary exam stage. Solving mock tests helps you limit your negative marks.

Along with studies, your routine, i.e., the timetable is also an essential part of the strategy for exam preparation. If you wish, you can follow the following timetable:

5:15 am to 6:15 am

Use this hour for exercise or light physical activity like a brisk walk. Meditation and yoga will relax your mind and relieve stress.

6:30 to 7:30 am

During this one hour, you should revise the topics studied on the previous day. That will lead to continuity for the subjects that you would study during the day today.

7:30 am to 8:00 am

Use this time to have breakfast and read newspapers. It will provide you with energy for the whole day. Reading newspapers will help you to be updated about national and international events. If possible, make notes of current affairs at the same time.

8:00 am to 10:30 am

This will be your first study session. At this time, you can study in a coaching class or at home. After this session, take an hour or two to rest.

11:30 am to 1:00 pm

This will be your second study session. During this, try to focus on the descriptive topics that you have to cover today.

1:00 pm to 1:30 pm

Have lunch. Include protein-rich foods in your diet. After this, if you want, you can take a break.

4:30 pm – 5:30 pm

This will be your third study session. At this time, study those topics which require more effort. After this, you can take a long break, during which you can do your personal work.

6:30 pm to 8:30 pm

This will be your fourth study session. By the evening, your mind will be somewhat stressed. That's why at this time, you can study your interesting subjects.

8:30 pm to 9:00 pm

It is dinner time. Avoid eating carbohydrates at night and include fruits and green vegetables for dinner.

9:00 pm to 10:00 pm

Watch English news and prime-time discussions on channels. They will provide you with an in-depth analysis of the top news stories of the day along with all the essential facts and figures.

After this, if you want, you can revise the topics studied throughout the day or prepare for sleep. Even after going to bed, you should try to revise in your mind what you had read during the day. With this, they will get imbibed well in your mind and you will be able to sleep easily.

Step-By-Step Preparation

Thousands of youths prepare for the IAS/IPS exams every year, but only a few achieve this goal. Although preparing for the IAS/IPS is very difficult with systematic preparation, the hope to achieve success in it increases.

Every year, lakhs of youth go through hard work for these posts. But by the third stage, i.e., the interview, many students have to face disappointment.

In this examination conducted by the UPSC, out of about four lakh students, only fifteen to twenty thousand students are able to cross the first stage. After that comes the main examination. At this stage, most of the students fall out of the race. Three times more students than the number of posts reach the last stage, i.e., interview, i.e., if applications have been invited for one thousand posts, then after the main examination about three thousand students appear for the interview. However, only a few people are successful in the interview. Very few students get the chance to serve as IAS officers. Other students join the IPS, Indian Foreign Service, and IRS, i.e., Indian Revenue Service or allied services.

The pattern of questions in the exam was changed with the thought that the students would be freed from the trap of coaching classes. But within a year, the coaching institutes gained dominance again. Now coaching institutes have also started coaching in preparation for CSAT. Experts say, 'In the current pattern when you prepare for the position of a collector, the preparation for the position of an inspector is also included.' That means the pattern of the exam has become such that it helps to a great extent in the preparation for banking services and Staff Selection Commission exams as well. There is no need for separate preparation for them.

Preparation by Making Pyramid

We should prepare for any exam by making a pyramid. In the initial phase, we should start our preparation by covering the syllabus. Then as the exam time approaches, to reach the top of the pyramid, one must prepare well from the syllabus. The preparation also depends on the core subjects of the syllabus.

Importance of Strategy

In any exam, strategy is important. The candidates who have been successful believe that one should prepare according to one's ability. While planning you need to see how many days you need for preparation. If you have a gap or interval in your exam, you can also reserve that time to prepare for the optional subject, and you can make good use of that extra time. If you use the time suitably, then you will not have any problem achieving success. If you prepare properly, you will be successful sooner. You can also prepare on the basis of the subjects in which the merit list is determined. However, do not ignore the subjects in which you can qualify.

Every Moment is Important

The candidates who have been successful in this exam believe that one can perform effectively in the main exam only when one makes good use of the extra or saved time. At this time, avoid reading new topics and rather revise what you have studied so far. Revision is the key to success. Apart from this, first of all, make a list of topics on which questions in the exam would be based and carry out your preparation according to this plan. If you feel that there is a gap in your GS paper, which can be completed in two days, then it will be better if you prepare for the GS paper first. Focus on other papers only after that. You will have to make such a plan yourself and implement it yourself. If you make this kind of plan for each subject, then you can be successful in using your extra time adequately.

Make Preparation Keeping the Gap in Mind

Successful people don't do anything different; rather they do everything in a different manner. If you want to score well in the main exam, you have to think out of the box to stand out from the crowd. First of all, check when the exam of your optional subject is. It is often seen that there is a gap of several days between two optional subjects. If this is the case with you too, then it would be better to prepare for your topics during the gap and use the remaining time for revision of other weak topics. This will give you some extra time to prepare for other subjects.

Focus on Compulsory Subject

Most of the candidates preparing for the IAS/IPS are not serious about preparing for General English and General Hindi. As a result of this, later they face many problems and owing to lack of time, they regret their strategy and luck at the last moment. Therefore, it is necessary to understand that all subjects have equal importance in the Union Public Service Commission examination. You cannot move ahead leaving a subject aside. If you secure qualifying marks in the compulsory subject, then only will other subjects be evaluated. That's why never make the mistake of taking them lightly. The best way is not to neglect General English and General Hindi which are of a qualifying nature and prepare them well.

Scientific Thinking Is Necessary

Many toppers who have cleared the mains believe that some students think that good marks can be scored in the essay even with less preparation. But it is not right to think so. You can score better marks in the essay only when you prepare for it in a scientific manner.

A better and ideal situation would be to decide on an area in advance wherein you will answer questions related only to that area. For example, if you decide earlier that you will write an essay on a politics-related topic only, then you will be in a better situation and you will also be successful in completing your preparation.

In this exam, there is a compulsory essay paper, in which you have to write an essay on any one topic in three hours. In this given time, you should write in a systematic and logical manner and also with imagination.

Notes from Coaching Classes Vs Standard Books for Preparation

Whenever preparation for the IAS/IPS exam is discussed, there is also a discussion about the study material. Students often face a dilemma about whether to read the books or the notes provided by the coaching centre for preparation. This dilemma sometimes confuses the students so much that they can neither focus on the books nor on the notes.

Coaching notes or traditional books - this dichotomy is not new in the case of the IAS/IPS exam. Advocates of both sides present their arguments and both parties are right in their respective positions. That's why it is natural for students to get confused.

One of the facts about the IAS/IPS exam preparation is that it is not possible to prepare for it without standard books. In fact, standard books provide a foundation for your preparation on which you build your knowledge. If you talk to any expert, they will advise you to read NCERT books first. There are many candidates who have continuously studied only NCERT books and have also been successful in the examination. Similarly, without reading M. Laxmikant's books on Polity, it can be extremely difficult to prepare for this subject. There are many subjects where only after studying from standard books, you can expand your knowledge and also develop the art of writing. In other words, preparations for some subjects like History, Polity, Geography, etc. should be done from standard books only.

But for the preparation of some subjects, you cannot find standard books in the market, such as environment, current affairs, etc. You have to depend on the notes for these topics. Essentially, there are some subjects in the UPSC where content is constantly updated. This is the reason why it is very difficult to find books for those subjects. So, you are left with only two options – either prepare your own notes by finding material from different sources or study from notes that you have got from reliable sources. Reputable coaching institutes can also be reliable sources. The advantage of the second option is that it saves your time and you do not need to read unnecessary news and material. For example, for notes on current affairs, you will have to read newspapers and magazines every day, extract useful news from them and make accurate notes from them. That would take too much time. But if someone else does the job for you, then all you have to do is remember them by reading them. This will save you both time and energy.

Some subjects in the syllabus for the IAS/IPS exam have fixed content, but it is also updated every year, like Science or Economics. Questions on these topics are based on standard content as well as the context of current affairs. For such subjects, you have to give equal importance to books and notes. In fact, it has been noticed in the changing pattern of the examination that the trend of questions is more oriented towards the present context. But you will be able to understand them only when you have basic knowledge of such topics. So, for these topics, first, you should strengthen your fundamentals by studying from standard books and then keep updating your knowledge with the help of notes.

As much as the syllabus of the IAS/IPS exam is comprehensive, its study material is much more detailed. And then in today's context, you cannot afford to depend on any one type of source. So, for the preparation, you have to strike a balance between the notes and the books.

Practice is Essential

The purpose of the essay paper is to test your thinking, language style, and ability to express yourself spontaneously. You need to practise extensively for this. Apart from this, if you have a friend or acquaintance who has already cracked the exam, then you can consult them and draw a strategy for preparation.

Increase Your Writing Capacity

A common problem faced by the students preparing for the UPSC exam is that though they study a lot they face many difficulties in question papers like essays due to a lack of writing practice. That's why experts advise that they should practise writing continuously. This writing practice will help you control your impulsive thoughts and express them systematically. Apart from this, essay writing is also supposed to be a continuous process. Herein, your style, mastery of language, point of view, and facts along with their sources are all checked. So, start practising from now on to have control over these factors.

Choose Core Area in All Subjects

Those people who have successfully cleared this exam, believe that you can get success in this exam only when you make your preparation fully according to the syllabus.

Your own notes are the best way to prepare well in less time. This is not our but the experts' opinion. Instead of getting caught in the pile of books, you should focus on the notes you prepared systematically throughout the year.

No matter how much you study, when it comes to covering an elaborate syllabus like the IAS/IPS, something important is bound to be missed at the last moment. So, it is better to keep some backup time as you give a final touch to the preparation. You can use this time to quickly browse through the topics that you missed.

Be Aware of the Limit of Words

Practise writing answers only in as many words as they are asked for, i.e., 'to the point'. The problem with students who do not follow this principle of the word limit is that in a bid to write long answers, they are unable to write the answers to other questions even after knowing them due to lack of time.

Studying Previous Question Papers

For the optional study, estimate the questions of the optional subject on the basis of previous years' papers and prepare their ideal answers. There are also sub-questions related to a question in the exam. So, keep in mind all the aspects related to it while preparing the answers to the estimated questions.

Maintain Balance in Writing

Remember, every word you write in the IAS/IPS exam reflects your ideology and personality. In such a situation, the inclination shown towards a particular policy or party can prove to be fatal for you here. So, take a balanced approach while writing answers and recognize the value of every word you write.

Revision is also Necessary

Candidates should get a hold on the subject of their interest and revise the selected subject. You should also practise writing the essay. If there is a problem related to orderliness, originality, and subject matter in the essay, then remove them. The syllabus of the first paper of General Studies is completely traditional. So, start working keeping that in mind.

Time Management is Critical

If you want to ensure your success in the main examination of Civil Services, then you should pay equal attention to all the question papers. You should not work hard on one paper and pay less attention to other papers. If you score maximum marks in all the papers, then your selection in the civil services will be assured to a great extent. So, it depends on how many marks you can score. The more marks you score in the mains exam, the surer will be your success in this exam.

While preparing, you also have to be aware of the time. It is essential to set a time limit for the preparation of all subjects so that no subject is left out. Similarly, while writing the exam, it is necessary to spend an equal amount of time on each question. It should not happen that you spend more time on any one question and then have to complete the rest of the questions in less time. So, remember that you should write the answers to those questions first which you know very well. Also, remember that you should answer each question in 35 minutes (optional question). Although it is important to focus on accuracy in the paper on General Studies you also need to focus on both speed and accuracy. Thus, solve the questions with awareness about the time limit.

Story of Success: Struggle is Success

Naveen Kumar Jha who was selected for the civil services is an example of struggle and success. Naveen was selected on his third attempt. He believes that if you are from an ordinary family, you have an ordinary background, you do not have sufficient resources, and you don't get success on the first attempt, then there is no need to worry and get disheartened. The Union Public Service

Commission will definitely give you a chance to be successful in the Civil Services. All that is required are patience and hard work.

Naveen, who was selected as an officer in the Railways through the Union Public Service Commission, overcame all the challenges faced by a middle-class family and succeeded. To meet his needs, he also gave tuition to children. Naveen says, "My family has played a pivotal role in my success, especially my elder brother, who is an export manager in a private company. My financial condition was deplorable. I come from a rural background, and yet my family members gave me adequate support." He cleared the preliminary examination on the first attempt, advanced to the interview stage on the second attempt, and finally on the third attempt, his diligence paid off and Naveen Kumar was selected. However, he did not get selected for the IAS due to his low rank. Even after his selection, he is busy preparing for the new exam. He believes that poverty and deprivation do not always hold one back, rather they also inspire. That means, if you have a passion for the civil service, then no challenge or problem comes in the way and success is yours.

❑

3

The Habit of Reading A Wide Range of Material

Many challenges occur during the service life of a civil servant working in an efficient and sound civil service system essential for the development of the country, which makes this service the most prestigious service in India.

As it is the highest level of service in India, the prestige attached to it and the various challenges it has, make this service more attractive, safe, and challenging. It is a powerful but social service-oriented job within the constitutional framework. It offers stability and the risks are less.

An IAS officer has a key role to play in policy matters. For example, under Article 77 of the Constitution, it is the duty of the Secretary of the Ministry or Department to ensure that the rules for the work mentioned for the executive of the Centre and the States under Article 166 are followed. Even if a minister issues an order which is against any rule, then it is the duty of the secretary to inform the minister about it. However, if the minister still insists on an illegal action, the file should be sent through the minister to the Prime Minister or the Chief Minister, as the case may be.

Administrative officers are the policymakers and implementers of the country. They represent the government in various countries or international fora. They are authorized to sign treaties on behalf of the government. When they work at the district level, they are known by popular titles such as DM, Collector, District Magistrate, etc. They are directly responsible for all kinds of work at the district level, be it development work, law and order, or disaster management. In secretariats, they perform the duties of Deputy Secretary, Under Secretary, Chief Secretary, Principal Secretary, etc. As officers, their best positions are in the form of Principal Secretary to the Prime Minister and Chief Ministers of various states.

Apart from being a bookworm, to be successful in the exam, you should also try to read different types of books. If you only like reading fiction, then you can read novels for some time to entertain yourself. But do not spend much time reading them, otherwise, it may become difficult for you to get success in the examination. But you should include different types of books in your study schedule and diversify your reading habit.

Watching Informative Programmes/Broadcasts

This is an important attribute for success in the IAS/IPS exam, which will help you immensely in your endeavour towards becoming an IAS/IPS officer. Many research studies have proved that humans learn more from the information presented in picture form than from plain text. Today, you will find many such TV channels. There are also older channels like Discovery and National Geographic, which can help you expand your knowledge on different topics. Apart from this, with a focus on India's diversity, these channels have also started airing India-centric shows and videos, which can give you a lot of new information about our country.

Using the Internet

We are living in the age of the internet. So, it is natural for IAS/IPS aspirants to rely on the Internet during exam preparation. Apart from the websites specially designed for the candidates, you can also use YouTube, Google News, Wikipedia, and other such websites or alternative sources. In fact, many successful IAS/IPS aspirants have found YouTube to be the best option among sources available to them to understand complex concepts and topics that have not been a part of their core education. For example, a student from a humanities background can understand thermodynamics very easily through videos. Similarly, Google News is one such source, which provides you with all the updates about events of national as well as international importance.

Best YouTube Channels for IAS/IPS Preparation

After the expansion of the internet throughout the world, the way of preparing for IAS/IPS has also changed considerably. The revolution brought about by YouTube has made human life very easy because every kind of information is available there for free. Because of all these benefits, nowadays candidates are drawn towards YouTube. But one problem with this is that there are too many channels, which often confuse the students as to which one to follow.

In the last few years, digital education has got a rapid boost in India. So, today it has become very easy for IAS/IPS aspirants to prepare for the exam from home. The best thing about online preparation is that students get diverse study material for free and they can use it at their convenience without any geographical restriction. However, you have to tread very carefully for the preparation of this exam. It is because nowadays, there are many mediums on the internet, which claim to be the best platform for the preparation of IAS/IPS, but in the end, they waste students' time. So, today, I will tell you about those few YouTube channels in Hindi, which can help you a lot in your preparation to make your dream of becoming an IAS/IPS officer come true.

Sansad TV

This channel is under the Government of India. On this channel, apart from the telecast of sessions in both Houses of Parliament, many programmes pertaining to other national and international matters are run. All aspects of political, economic, social and cultural life are highlighted on this channel in great depth in which experts participate. This is a very important channel for students to prepare for the Civil Services Examination.

Press Information Bureau, Government of India

This is the main agency that provides information about the policies and achievements of the Central Government. It conveys information to newspapers and electronic media through press releases, press conferences, interviews, and press briefings. It is very important for preparation regarding current affairs for any government exam.

Drishti IAS

'Drishti the Vision' is run by Vikas Divyakirti, a 1996 batch IAS officer. It has been one of the most preferred coaching institutes for IAS/IPS aspirants for the last two decades. It is known for providing easy access to video classes, audio-visual notes, and other content to the candidates according to the syllabus, which proves effective from the preliminary exam to interview.

Unacademy

Unacademy was started in the year 2015 by former IAS officer Dr. Roman Saini. This institute has achieved a unique position in a very short span of time. Unacademy helps prepare for all government exams and has also started a separate YouTube channel to help Hindi students.

Vision IAS

'Vision IAS Coaching Institute' runs separate YouTube channels in both Hindi and English languages. On this channel, many toppers address sessions to motivate the candidates and tell them about excellent ways of preparation. This channel is also useful for preparing for every stage of the exam.

Prabhat Exam

Although most of you are aware of this channel, for those who do not know, let me tell you that this is a channel where you get information about every aspect of IAS/IPS preparation. Here, you will also find inspiring stories and knowledge-based videos. You will also find interviews of toppers, which will help you to draw a strategy for your preparation.

Travelling

There is an old saying – 'There is no better way to learn than to travel', and it is completely true when it comes to the IAS exam. If you are fond of travelling and you like to visit new and interesting places, then it can teach you a lot about the history, culture, and even geography of the place. Travelling brings about a change in your perspective by adding or changing many new things in your knowledge about different places. For most of the IAS aspirants living in the northern region, knowing Mughal history can be easy. All you need to do is visit the popular forts and other places mentioned in the course. A visit to the Red Fort will teach you more about its history than reading a hundred pages. Similarly, if you want to know about the topography of the Aravalli hills, then going there in person will be most effective. One of the best learning experiences is a trip to the seven states of the North-East - the Seven Sisters - to get a better more comprehensive understanding of the region's vastly different culture and traditions.

Developing Creativity

In fact, creative people do not see things as they are, rather they see things as they could be. If you aspire to become an IAS/IPS, officer, then creativity should be one of the success mantras in your life. As an IAS/IPS officer, you will be expected to deal with several different situations and take tough decisions with some creativity and out of the box thinking. In short, your main responsibility will be to understand the intricate things and come up with simple yet creative solutions to complex problems. Your abilities are also tested during the IAS/IPS exam. So, in fact, creative thinking can also help you create new preparation strategies to crack the IAS/IPS exam. Creative thinking will help you to become a successful officer.

Critical Thinking

Like creativity, critical thinking is also very important for an IAS/IPS aspirant. IAS/IPS officers are well-versed in the bureaucratic structure of the country. Many may disagree with this, but this quality will work in your favour as a candidate. Since most of the syllabus for the IAS/IPS exam contains events from our daily life, you just need to think critically about them to understand the perspective.

Most of the information available today is the result of critical thinking, common questions about people and activities. Similarly, if you can critically examine and analyse concepts and relate them to your daily life, it will help you understand concepts in detail and answer questions in the exam. So, start acting as per Sherlock's maxim - 'Stop watching and start scrutiny today'.

Appropriate Use of Time

Right from our school days, we have been told to be 'punctual'. Many of us have accepted it and made it a part of our lifestyle. But there are still people who are unable to manage their time.

If you are among the second type of people, then you have to be more cautious as it can seriously affect your chances of cracking the IAS/IPS exam. Time is the scarcest resource for an IAS aspirant. Hence, being punctual and managing time properly is important for cracking the exam. On the other hand, it prepares the candidates for the disciplined life that they have to lead after clearing the exam.

Commitment and Self-Motivation

Cracking the IAS/IPS exam is not easy as there are lakhs of aspirants competing for a few hundred seats. Things get worse over time when you are unable to study because of personal or health issues. When you are unable to study because of personal or health issues, the circumstances become tougher in terms of time. Sometimes you need strength and inspiration to read bulky reference books. If you are a committed self-motivated person who wants to crack IAS/IPS exam, then it will become very easy for you. Inculcating commitment and self-motivation play a vital role in cracking the IAS/IPS exam.

Fewer Resources, More Revision

First of all, remember that preparation for the preliminary examination, main examination, and interview should be done together and not separately. Frequently, the questions that appear in the preliminary exam also appear in the main exam. That's why revision is necessary. You cannot achieve success only by collecting extensive study material, it also has to be studied and memorized. You should take mock tests. Simultaneously, increase the speed of writing by practising answer writing.

First Target the Preliminary Exam

The preliminary examination should be your first target. If you do not cross this hurdle, then all further preparation will go in vain.

Preparation for both exams should be carried out simultaneously since later there will be no time to prepare for the main exam. But initially, the focus should remain on the preliminary exam. Keep checking your revision through mock tests.

Don't Be Discouraged, Be Patient

The most essential things required to crack this exam are patience and perseverance. Prepare your mind in such a way that you will study especially well on the day that you don't feel like studying and see how new courage arises in you. Stay connected with people from whom you derive inspiration and positive energy. It is better to keep away from people with negative thoughts. Failure or success - both are in our minds and we can achieve anything if we set our mind to it.

The Habit of Using Time Appropriately

One of the most important habits is managing and using time appropriately. Candidates should know how to manage their time. They should make a habit of planning the preparation for the exam before actually starting the preparation for the exam so that they have enough time to cover the entire syllabus properly. They should make a clear study plan covering all the subjects and follow it.

Important Topics and Revision

Since there is a vast syllabus for the exam and studying different books simultaneously can cause confusion, you should not read too many books or study from different books. You should practise selective reading and pay more attention to those topics from the syllabus which are important. To avoid confusion, it is better to read only 1-2 good books on each subject. Also, you must inculcate the habit of revision.

UPSC - Preliminary Exam (More the Practice Better the Score)

Close your eyes and for a moment, imagine that you are about to enter the examination hall. There are hundreds of people around you, but you are unaware of them. You have only one thought in your mind – today is the day you are about to enter the battlefield and the world is looking at you. Today is the test of your hard work, your patience, and your future. Do you feel like a cricketer? A player on whom hundreds of eyes are fixed and for whom thousands of people are praying for an exemplary performance. Just like cricket, only those who have sweated it out practising can perform creditably on the UPSC pitch.

As important as studying to qualify for the IAS/IPS is utilizing that study in 2 hours during the exam. Therefore, it is very important to understand how best time management, mental concentration, and brain activity can be made possible in those 2 hours. As soon as you occupy your seat in the examination hall, make your mind completely calm. Forget the pressure of the crowd and focus all your energy on just one point. There will be multiple questions (overs) in succession. So, prepare yourself to solve one question after another (play shots).

The total number of questions in the General Studies paper of the preliminary examination is 100, which have to be solved in just 2 hours or 120 minutes. In that sense, the examinees get just 72 seconds for each question, and everyone knows the level of complexity and depth of the questions. Do not start solving questions immediately after getting the question paper, rather go through the entire paper and try to understand it, i.e., see how many questions have been asked from various topics, and how difficult or easy they are. With this, your mind will understand the strength of the opposing army (question paper) at the beginning of the war (match). If you have done a lot of net practice (i.e., you have taken many mock tests), it will automatically benefit you.

The candidate has to darken the correct circle in the answer sheet by selecting the correct option from the options given in the question within 72 seconds. In such a situation, there is a danger of marking wrong answers. It also takes more time to solve the questions due to difficult options. Sometimes students are not even able to read the entire paper. Suffice it is to say that the nature of questions in the IAS/IPS exams is so deep and the options so complex that time management becomes a challenge. The way to deal with this challenge is to first attempt only those questions which are within the range of the examinee's knowledge. Those questions whose answers you do not know or you are doubtful about should be marked and left for the time being and if time is left at the end, try to answer them. Otherwise, it is better to leave them.

The exam expects the candidate to use the correct technique to solve the questions by taking a 'calculative risk'. Let us understand the method of 'Calculative Risk' to solve the question paper in this manner.

Avoid guessing where you do not know the answer at all, i.e., when you cannot think of any option in the question to be correct. It is better to skip such questions to save time.

When you know about any one of the four options given in the question, but have no idea about the remaining three options. At that time, on the basis of the calculative risk, you should try to answer such questions. This will ultimately benefit the candidates in terms of marks. But it would be better to answer such questions in the remaining time after solving the rest of the questions.

If you know about two out of the four options given in a question and do not know about the other two, then the answer must be given on the basis of supposition. If you do this in 6 questions and assuming that according to 50 per cent probability, you get 3 questions right and 3 wrong, then you will get an advantage of 4 marks, which is very important from the point of view of success.

As a part of the technique of solving questions, candidates should always proceed gradually from 'easy-questions' to 'complex-questions' while understanding the nature of the questions. Also, the 'elimination method' should be used in the questions whose answers are not directly known to them. Under the elimination method, one has to gradually reach the correct answer by leaving those options out of the four options which are most likely to be wrong. This method is very effective, so it must be used during the exam.

Success Story: Success Without Coaching

Shubham Kumar of Katihar topped the IAS 2020 final exam and became an example for the youth of not only Bihar but across the country. It is generally said that about 18 to 20 hours of study is required for the preparation of the IAS exam. But Shubham achieved this feat by studying for only 7 to 8 hours.

Shubham says that he started preparing for the IAS in the year 2018. But during this time, he also went through numerous ups and downs. However, he maintained the focus and attempted as much as he could. The period during the Corona pandemic was very difficult, but he was strongly determined to prepare for the exam. He received tremendous support from his family.

Shubham studied in Purnia and Katihar and then in Patna. He passed his 12th exam from Bokaro. He then graduated in Civil Engineering from Mumbai IIT. Shubham observes that when he was in the sixth standard, an incident happened, after which he decided to study in Patna. It so happened that when he studied in Class VI in Katihar, one of his answers was marked wrong by his teacher. Shubham felt that his answer was correct, and he was deeply hurt when the teacher declared it wrong. Then he decided to change schools. He then moved to Patna.

Shubham did not take any coaching for the IAS preparation and studied for 7 to 8 hours a day. After clearing the preliminary exam, he started studying for 8 to 10 hours. According to Shubham's mother, he was good in studies from the beginning. Shubham has been a topper since childhood.

❑

4

Simple Ways to Earn Excellent Marks

In the main exam of IAS/IPS, apart from hard work, scoring subjects are also very important. This is the reason why some topics are always 'hot' in the main examination. Apart from other subjects in the Civil Services Main Examination, a number of students opt for philosophy as a second option as a scoring subject. According to experts, philosophy is not only a scoring subject but its syllabus is also much shorter than other subjects. If you are interested in philosophy and you have also selected this subject in the main examination, you can score better marks in this subject with a slight effort.

Study the Syllabus

According to the main examination, the syllabus of Philosophy is broadly divided into the following three sections – History and Problems of Philosophy, Socio-Political Philosophy, and Religious Philosophy. It is from these three sections that two papers on Philosophy are designed for the main examination. Therefore, on the basis of the nature of the question paper, they can be divided into subsections. Western philosophy and Indian philosophy are included under the History and Problems of Philosophy.

To facilitate the study, Western philosophy is divided into Traditional Western philosophy (related to rationalism and empiricism) and Contemporary Western philosophy (philosophy related to language analysis). In this way, the first question paper is designed by combining Western philosophy and Indian philosophy, while the second question paper is designed from socio-political philosophy and religious philosophy.

Preparation According to the Syllabus

The first question paper on Philosophy includes a total of 11 philosophers and their selected theories under the Western Philosophy syllabus. Of these, the first five are traditional Western philosophers and the remaining six are linguistic analytical philosophers. A total of 9 philosophers and their selected theories have been included in the section on Indian philosophy. In the second question paper, 10 topics on socio-political philosophy and religious philosophy each are included in the syllabus.

Up-to-Date Information

Since 2008, a radical change has been made to the syllabus of philosophy. Earlier in traditional Western philosophy, different philosophers and some of their selected philosophical theories were included. But now philosophers and theories have been added to the syllabus in the form of a philosophical style. In contemporary Western philosophy, the philosophical theories of succeeding Wittgenstein and Heidegger have found a place in the new curriculum. In Indian philosophy, contemporary philosopher Aurobindo's principles such as development, counter-development and complete yoga have been added to the new syllabus. Some topics have been removed from socio-political philosophy and new topics have been added. In general, no change has been made to the syllabus of religious philosophy.

CSAT has brought students from all the streams to the same level. This has helped to eliminate the tendency of cramming and see the rationality, understanding, personality, and administrative qualities of the candidate. In this situation, the candidate's thinking, thought processes, mastery of language, decision-making ability in different situations, and ability to assess and calculate at a fast pace is revealed. CSAT is divided into several parts. There is a strategy for each part-

Language - Hindi/English

In the first part of CSAT, questions are given in both Hindi and English. In this part, questions are based on prose passages. You should read the passage carefully, understand it well and then only answer the questions. You should answer the questions based on the passage in the language you (the candidate) have opted for instead of the language in your form. If you have opted for Hindi, read the Hindi passage and answer the questions.

Mathematics

In CSAT, your precision will be checked through Mathematics. Under Maths, there will be questions from NCERT (6-10) Maths book up to Class 10, like percentage, average, age and work, time and distance, probability, etc. Maths questions can be simplified with precision in less time by practising them several times. You have to memorize a few things like squares from 1 to 50 and square roots from 1 to 10, etc. It is essential to keep your mind firm while solving the questions.

Decision-Making Capacity

Decision-making is the main function of the administrator. A good decision ends a problem forever. While taking any decision, information, and data related to the problem are analysed which shows your knowledge, understanding, patience, ability to take the initiative, etc. Therefore, solve these types of questions by dividing them into several steps. Through the questions related to a sudden problem, the decision-making capacity of a common man or administrator and the ability to assess the circumstances with precision, etc. are tested. While taking decisions, it is necessary for him/her to take humanity, the constitution, legislation, etc. into consideration.

For example, if you get information about a bomb in a mall, then you have to provide the specific information to the manager and slowly get the mall evacuated.

Communication Skills

A public servant has to talk to the public, politicians, media, and bureaucrats. Therefore, every public servant should have the quality of establishing contact/communication/negotiations with different persons at different times. An administrator's communication is fact-based. Therefore, none of his statements should hurt the respect of the Constitution, the Court, the Legislature or the public. It is always necessary for them to establish direct, simple, easy and concise communication. Care should also be taken to ensure that all communication is established through formal channels.

Reasoning Ability

In this part, mainly the mental power of the candidate is tested. Most of the questions are in the form of puzzles, which have to be solved. For this, R.S. Aggarwal's book is very useful. It contains many types of questions such as puzzles, etc. With more practice, questions can be solved in less time.

Mental Ability

This is also a part of the reasoning test in a way. An incident has to be proved on the basis of the data given. For this also, the book by R.S. Aggarwal is useful.

English Language and Comprehension Test

This part is in English only for all the candidates. In this, some passage-based questions are asked. Read the passage carefully and answer the questions. Some questions in this section are also based on grammar, for which any grammar book of Class 10 is useful. For the preparation of this part, practise repeatedly on the question papers of other multiple-choice examinations conducted by the Union Public Service Commission, in which English questions are asked. This will give you an idea of the nature of the question and will also help you in the exam.

CSAT is a boon for those candidates who lay emphasis on understanding rather than rote learning. Through this, in the near future, the country will get bureaucrats with reasoning and analytical abilities.

Attention

Maintain consistency in the hours spent on studying. Instead of studying for 14 hours one day and 2 hours the next day, study for 10 hours daily.

Study in a group. Doubts will also be cleared quickly by this and studying will be enjoyable. Make a goal for each day and meet it.

Follow these 5 rules - reading, writing, listening, speaking, and logical argument - to master the language.

The scope of IAS/IPS is huge. Officers can be posted in any field. So, go through each and every topic related to general events in depth.

Read NCERT books to understand the core of the subject and always keep your focus on the goal.

Importance of Diagrams in the IAS/IPS Preparation

It is true that what we cannot understand through words, we can easily understand through pictures. For example, to explain something about a poor man, many examples and circumstances have to be cited. But if we draw a correct picture, then we can easily understand the many problems and circumstances of that poor man in one stroke and can also explain them to others. The same is the case with the diagrams in the preparation for the IAS/IPS.

If you are preparing for the UPSC preliminary exam, you would know that studying maps is an integral part of exam preparation. Maps-related questions are asked in the preliminary exam and it is also an important aspect of the optional paper on geography in the main exam. Generally, you can expect 9 to 10 questions from the Maps section in the preliminary exam. As we know that in earlier exams candidates were given blank maps and had to mark places, etc. on them. But at present, maps are not given; only the names of places are given in the questions and you have to arrange them in the correct order. So, your understanding and knowledge of maps should be clear. Some candidates believe that part of the maps can also be learned by rote like other subjects, but it is wrong. We have to understand that a candidate requires a strategic understanding of maps to tackle the map-related questions asked in the UPSC exam.

Now the question arises how should one study for the maps? For that, you can follow these tips –

Learn about all the neighbouring countries of India. Name the various Indian states which share their borders with such neighbouring countries and give more importance to the countries in the Indian subcontinent.

For the peninsular part of India and the oceanic area around the islands in the Indian Ocean, study the map of India thoroughly, for example, the extension of Andaman and Nicobar Islands, countries closest to Lakshadweep Islands, different channels - 10°, 9°, etc.

You should study the important latitudinal and longitudinal lines on the map of India. For example, you should study the states through which the Tropic of Cancer passes.

Apart from this, you should also study the 'hypothesis-based' lines, the nature of the shores, etc. For example, learn about the division of India based on the 10°C isotherm.

You should be able to draw a political map of India (an outline) by hand (which is very important for General Studies Paper-I and General Studies Paper-II in Mains). You should know which states share their borders with how many and with which states.

Study all the prominent cities on the map of India. You should be able to indicate them and also be able to find out which city is in the west/east/north/south of a particular city.

You should draw on the map the source or origin, course of flow and tributaries of all the rivers of India. For example, to arrive at a correct answer to a question asked in the preliminary examination, knowledge about the river Teesta was required.

You should note the range and important peaks of all mountain ranges - both Himalayan and Peninsular. You should be able to draw the entire mountain range on a topographic map of India and show the highest peak in it.

Study the locations of various glaciers located north of the Vindhyas and also note the various rivers originating from these mountain ranges/glaciers.

For any important recent news, you should look for important places in the Atlas. Learn about national borders and bordering countries.

Studying maps is not an extra task and can be done as a recreational activity during your study break. By drawing mind maps of India and the world, a substantial part of current affairs, geography, world history, economy, etc. can be studied very easily and will help greatly in understanding them. Being able to draw good maps and locate important places/features will be very useful to you, especially in GS-1 Geography/History and GS-3 Economics.

Success Story: From Nursing to IAS

A farmer from a village in Kerala had a dream. His dream was that his daughter should become an IAS officer. With this dream, he gave the best education to his daughters and his daughter also made his dream come true.

The girl who made her father's dream come true is Annies Kanmani Joy, who managed to crack the Civil Services Examination 2012. Annie Kanmani Joy not only cleared the exam in 2012 but also secured 65th rank.

Annies had not done this for the first time. Annies also passed the civil service exam in 2011. Then her rank was 580. Based on that, Annies went in for officer training under the Indian Accounts Service.

In response to the question as to how she was inspired to become an IAS officer, Annies says, "My father had shown me this dream since childhood. However, I did not prepare for it since childhood. I prepared for this exam after the internship."

Annies is the first nurse who managed to clear the Civil Services Examination. Little did she know that if she passed the exam, she would be the first woman to do so. In response to this question, Annies says, "When I started preparing, I thought that I should consult an IAS nurse. But I could not find one. I got to know about this fact only after clearing the exam."

" Rural background does not matter much. What matters is how much passion you have. And then I am from Kerala, where education is considered very important. It may be a big deal for you that a village girl has accomplished something great. But all this seems simple to me."

When asked what her father said about the news, Annies says, "When I told my father on the phone, he was speechless, though I can understand his joy."

Annies specially mentioned one particular aspect. She said, "My father believes that education is the real wealth that we can give to our daughter. Even though we belong to a farmer's family, he gave me the best education. Another trend in Kerala is that parents definitely send their children to school."

Annies admits that she studied nine hours a day for the past two years. When asked if she felt she missed anything in the past two years, Annies said, "Maybe I missed some social events or get-togethers, but nothing much."

❑

5

Strategy, Discipline and Patience

Becoming an IAS/IPS officer can be everyone's dream, but it takes hard work and struggle to become an IAS/IPS officer. To be successful in civil services, it is very important to have strategy, discipline, and patience.

The Constitution, underlining the importance of civil services in the concept of ideal administration, gives administrative officers the key to restoring order in every corner of the country. Whatever may be the project of development, whatever may be the draft of public welfare, however difficult the moments of natural calamity may be, the first response comes from the administration. In such a situation, it is not an exaggeration to say that the development of the country starts with efficient administration.

You may have seen people around you in trouble and often your heart must have been filled with their pain. You may have been troubled by a question as to how to solve their problems. Indian Administrative Service – this is a rational answer to this question that is lurking in your mind. While working in this position, you can use your authority to resolve the sufferings of your compatriots and their daily problems. No other work gives this kind of satisfaction.

Why the success percentage in IAS/IPS exam is only 0.2 per cent?

Often, you must have heard that it is one of the toughest exams not only in India but in the world. Some people even consider it to be the toughest exam in the world. The level of competition in the exam is very high. But is it so high that 99.9 per cent of applicants fail? Well, it is true that this test is tough. But most of the aspirants' own mistakes lead them to failure.

As we mentioned that only 0.2 per cent of the candidates crack this prestigious and tough exam. But it does not mean that 0.2 per cent of candidates have some extraordinary skills. However, they are definitely different and smarter than other candidates who could not crack this exam.

We have compiled a list of some of the reasons why IAS/IPS aspirants fail the exam. Let us take a look at it.

Easy syllabus is a trap

If you have applied for the exam for the first time and you think that the syllabus for prelims is not too difficult, let me warn you that the IAS/IPS syllabus for the exam is like an iceberg. The syllabus of the Civil Services Examination is endless. If you delay your preparation by simply looking at the syllabus, then you are not going to get success in the preliminary exam, too.

Ignoring NCERT Books

Conceptual knowledge is essential to crack the main exam and for that NCERT books are the best option. Many candidates ignore these books and some of them also prefer to other books by famous authors. Though these books enhance your knowledge, your foundation of the subjects will be developed by NCERT books only. Although NCERT books should not be the only study material chosen for IAS preparation, you should include them in your study material.

Lack of proper planning and guidance

Another reason for failure in the UPSC exam is lack of planning. In an exam like the IAS, where the level of competition is very high, even a single mark can change your result. Planning for exam preparation plays a crucial role. Many students make a single subject so difficult for themselves that all their energy and time goes into preparing for that subject and they do not score well in others. Some students make a plan but are unable to stick to it. That's why they fail this exam. Planning is not about time table alone, rather in the context of the examination, it is about making a plan to prepare all the topics from the syllabus within a stipulated time. So, aspirants should make a plan and stick to it.

Not taking a mock test or test series

There are many mock test series available on various sites on the internet for free or for a very nominal fee. When you solve these mock test series, you actually test your knowledge, and you are aware of your weaknesses and strengths. Another and most important advantage of these mock tests is that they help you with time management.

Lack of passion

Before choosing the IAS as your career option, you should think about why you want to become IAS/IPS - for yourself or for your parents, or for any other reason. It may sound strange, but the truth is that one's passion is what motivates one the most to crack any exam. If you appear for the exam just to please someone, it will be difficult for you to succeed. Fame, money, respect, and comfortable life are associated with the post of IAS/IPS and if you are appearing for the exam because of any one of them, then you are not on the wrong track. However, your passion should be to clear the exam. Everything else will follow in your life after you succeed in this exam.

How Important is Coaching?

IAS/IPS exam is considered very important in our country. For this, candidates often prefer opting for the coaching. By doing so, they feel that they will easily pass this exam. But to really pass this exam, coaching is not required. What is required is hard work along with goal setting, time management, patience, and dedication, only after which this exam can be cleared. Since candidates have more faith in taking coaching for exam preparation, they consider joining the most expensive coaching classes in the city as the success mantra, whereas this should not be the first plan of the aspirant who starts the preparation. You can prepare for the exam even by staying at home.

UPSC (IAS/IPS) Preparation at Home

Although no time can be set for success in any examination, with 18 months of tireless hard work and firm resolve, the UPSC aspirant can reach this goal. But for this, the candidate has to keep a keen eye on all the social-economic-global events including current affairs because the goal of the IAS/IPS exam can be achieved only by crossing the three stages. The first stage is called the preliminary exam, in which questions related to current affairs and subjects are asked. Even if the student is left with 60 days, it is not impossible to reach the target with the right strategy and sheer grit.

One-Year Study Plan for Self-Study

After the corona pandemic in 2020, our way of life has changed to a great extent. Earlier also self-study used to be important for the candidates, but now they have started believing in it even more. In such a situation, if you want, you can qualify for the UPSC exam on the basis of self-study by making a good study schedule and plan.

Prepare Yourself

How should you start UPSC preparation at home? Before you attempt to understand this, you must prepare yourself for this journey. Before starting the preparation for the exam, you should prepare yourself mentally and physically. Then you should set goals and devote time effectively.

Make a precise timetable

To become an IAS/IPS officer, your routine needs to be like that of an officer with a well-organized daily routine. Before preparation, you should set a timetable and stick to it. Making a timetable will make your preparation easier and more organized than before. By sticking to the deadline, you will be able to work better and complete the syllabus faster. Analyse the topics covered in the syllabus and understand your strengths and weaknesses.

The most important thing is to understand the entire syllabus of the exam thoroughly. But it is not necessary for you to have a complete understanding of the syllabus on the very day you are planning to start preparing for the exam. What is meant by the analysis of the syllabus is that you should be able to decide about the information related to the subjects and points that you have to keep in mind, and which subjects have been included in your examination.

Along with this, you will also have to collect the appropriate study material. By carefully analysing the syllabus and studying the previous year's questions, you will get an idea of where to obtain the right study material.

After going through the exam syllabus and old question papers and collecting relevant study material, now it is time to make the best and easy self-study plan for yourself. For this, some important things should be kept in mind. They are as follows –

While making a plan for self-study, first of all, decide how much time is left for the exam. If there is sufficient time, do not make a very rigid study plan.

As far as possible, the self-study plan should be made bearing in mind the necessary daily activities like exercise, outside chores, etc.

While making a plan, one must cover each and every part of the entire syllabus. You can allocate more or less time to different parts of the syllabus. But the strategy of not including a certain part in the plan with the intention of covering it later can prove risky because we do not know about the situations that will arise later and sometimes, we are not able to cover that part of the syllabus till the exam. Therefore, it is necessary to include each part of the syllabus in the study plan and allocate time to it as per the requirement.

While making a self-study plan, we should also try to make it practical. Frequently, when we draw up a self-study plan or timetable, according to it, we immediately set the time for the next subject after studying one subject. When we do this, we are not able to follow the timetable over a long period of time because this plan is not practical. So, while making a study plan, you should not make a plan for more than 1 hour at a stretch.

Allocate a maximum of 45 to 60 minutes to different parts of the syllabus and take a gap of at least 10 minutes before starting the next subject or topic. During that gap, you can do various activities for your entertainment.

Preparation for UPSC (IAS/IPS) After the 10th Standard

Even though one cannot appear for the UPSC exam after the 10th standard, one can start preparing for it –

- First of all, it is necessary to have complete knowledge about the exam.
- One should understand the syllabus of the exam.
- Collect strategy and study material.

- Study with concentration.
- Along with studies, writing is also necessary.
- Take mock tests repeatedly.
- Read newspapers and magazines daily.

Success does not come easily to anyone, especially to IAS/IPS aspirants. To achieve any kind of success, students have to work hard day and night. Along with this, they have to adopt such habits in their life, which will give them success in every field.

What stream should one opt for after the 10th class to become an IAS/IPS officer? Arts or Science?

Nowadays, due to the cutthroat competition seen among the youth, everyone is getting serious about their career at a very young age. In such a situation, many candidates are confused as to which stream they should opt for after their 10th standard to become an IAS/IPS so that along with school or college studies, they can start preparing for the exam as soon as possible.

We all know that till Class 10 in school, we have to study all the subjects together. After the completion of the 10th standard, students have to choose any one stream from the science, commerce, or arts streams. After that, in Classes 11 and 12, they study the subjects under that stream. You can become an IAS/IPS with any stream or subject. All they need is to work hard and prepare for the exam so that by passing it, their dream of becoming an IAS/IPS becomes a reality.

Which subjects you should opt for depends on your interest. If you are interested in science, then you should complete your 11th and 12th standard with science and after that prepare for the IAS/IPS. If you are interested in finance and the economy, then you can study commerce.

Which candidates should choose science subject?

If you have an interest in science and want to undertake further studies in science and you also want to become an IAS/ IPS officer, then you should opt for science in the 11th and 12th standards.

After studying science, you can also choose fields like engineering, medicine, or research. In case you fail the UPSC exam, you can make a decent career in this field. This is the biggest advantage of studying science - you can have a bright future in engineering and the medical field as well.

Which students should opt for the commerce subject?

If you are really interested in the economics and finance fields, then you can opt for the commerce subject in your 11th and 12th standards.

After studying the commerce subject, you have many more options. For example, you can become a CA and you can also work in the income tax department.

If for some reason you fail the IAS/IPS exam, you can get a job in any field of finance or tax department. Since you have prepared for the UPSC exam, cracking any other exam would not be that difficult for you.

As you would have studied well, you would easily get a job in the finance and income tax departments and you can build a good future for yourself.

Which students should choose the Arts stream?

If you are interested in subjects like History, Geography, and Political Science, then you can opt for Arts subjects for your 11th and 12th standards. More questions are asked on these topics in the

Civil Services Examination. If you study Arts in the 11th and 12th, it will help you immensely in preparing for the IAS/IPS exam.

By studying Arts subjects well, you will be able to focus better on the IAS/IPS exam during your 11th and 12th standards itself because the subjects you have to study for the preparation of this exam are the same subjects that you will study in the Arts stream.

So, if you want to become an IAS/IPS officer and you have keen of interest in subjects like History and Geography, then you can choose Arts subjects for the 11th and 12th. It will help you in your preparation to become an IAS/IPS.

In all the examinations conducted for government jobs, most of the questions are asked from the subjects in the Arts stream. So, choosing the arts stream will help you in other exams for government jobs.

Preparation for the UPSC exam along with school-college studies

Looking at the way today's youth are attracted to the UPSC exam, it would not be wrong to say that the sooner you start preparing for it, the better. Although the requirement to appear for this exam is graduation, if one waits till graduation to prepare for it, then one will be left behind in the race at the beginning itself. So, today we will talk about how to prepare for the IAS/IPS during school and college days.

During our school days, we start getting an idea of what we want to become in the future. Serious students start preparing for their future right from their school days. Hence, students who want to become civil servants in the future should start their preparation during the school days itself.

The best time is after you pass your 10th class examination. First of all, you must understand the UPSC exam pattern and read its syllabus thoroughly. After understanding all this, make a strategy for this exam in advance and collect the study material. From the

10th class, you should make a habit of reading newspapers and also the magazines related to this exam because it is necessary to keep studying them continuously for questions on current affairs in the exam. The earlier you get used to it, the better. Along with studies, the practice of writing is also necessary. Keep practising it in advance and if you want, you can start taking mock tests from the 10th class onwards. With this, you get to know about the syllabus as well as exam patterns, etc. In this way, continuously preparing for it can make it easier to crack the UPSC exam. For this exam, we have to study with a lot of hard work and dedication. That's why we should plan a routine for our studies so that we can spend our day in a systematic way. Having a routine helps a lot in your studies. From time to time, keep reminding yourself about the tasks you have to carry out at particular hours. When you follow a routine, you are able to use your time in a systematic and methodical way.

Now it is time for college after the 12th class examination. The things which are necessary for UPSC exam preparation from the 10th Class onwards, almost the same things are applicable for exam preparation after the 12th class as well. After the 12th class exam, you enrol for graduation. There you should choose those subjects which are optional subjects in the UPSC exam syllabus. Preparing for a prestigious exam like the Indian Administrative Services is no less than an adventure. So, you should not ignore your responsibility during your graduation. UPSC appreciates good graduation grades. The subjects you choose during your graduation can come in handy during the interview round. You should concentrate fully on the syllabus related to the subject you have chosen at the graduation level. This will help you in preparing for the optional subjects you choose.

You should also practise writing along with studying because after clearing the preliminary exam, you have to appear for the main exam, which involves extensive writing. So, try to write about 200 words on any topic. The more you practise writing, the more your writing style will improve and you will make fewer grammatical mistakes.

Undergraduate students get the full three years. Therefore, you should use these years well. The whole syllabus can be studied by making a plan so that after graduation, success in the IAS/IPS exam can be achieved during postgraduation itself.

Study Difficult Topics First

Everyone has their own favourite and non-favourite subjects. It has been observed that the students tend to study the subjects they like more and ignore the difficult subjects, which they should not do. One quality of successful students is that they pay more attention to difficult subjects. They first start studying difficult subjects and study easy topics later.

Making Notes is Necessary

Notes are an important factor in clearing the UPSC exam. Without proper and effective notes, it will be challenging for you to move ahead in your preparation. You should try to make notes with proper analysis through information obtained from authentic sources. These notes will be helpful in your exam preparation as you will not be able to go through the whole material again due to lack or shortage of time. There are many other exams for various government jobs, but they are not as challenging as the IAS/IPS exam. So, preparing for this exam requires a great effort.

Successful students have a secret. They ensure to make notes while studying. There are several benefits to making notes. While making notes, you remember more than half of the subject and on revising, you remember everything well. As a result, you score good marks in the exam. So, if you want to be a successful student, you should also make notes.

Study According to the Syllabus

Another secret of successful students is that they always study according to the syllabus. When you study according to the syllabus, no subject gets left out and the syllabus is also completed on time.

Set Time for Study

You should study daily at a fixed time. You can make your own schedule. If you want, you can study from 5 to 9 in the morning, from 12 to 3 in the afternoon, and from 5 to 9 in the evening. There is no time as such for studying. Though you can study anytime it is advisable to study at a fixed time.

Regular Studies

Most of the students study exhaustively in the beginning, but within a few months, their enthusiasm wanes. Then they stop studying for 15 days or 1-2 months or study very little. This habit found in many students is not correct. You should avoid this. If you want to crack the UPSC exam, you must study regularly.

If you plea to appear for any kind of examination, then mock tests are very important for you. You must take a mock test every month to be successful in the exam. It is also called a practice set. By solving these, you get to know how much you recall from what you studied.

Learn from Mistakes

You should learn from your mistakes. For example, you scored very good marks in some subjects in the previous exam but you scored less marks in maths, because of which you could not get selected. So, next time you should work harder in maths and pass that exam. This is called learning from your mistakes.

Learn About Course Material

The core of any exam is its syllabus. Before you start reading books, you must first understand the syllabus. This will enable you decide what is essential for studying and what can be overlooked. Since the questions in all the exams are from the given syllabus, it is imperative to constantly check the syllabus. Thus, it is important for all freshers to understand the preliminary stage syllabus and exam pattern. The UPSC has provided a detailed syllabus for the preliminary and main examinations of CSE. Students must also be aware of the eligibility criteria to take the exam.

Solve Previous Years' Question Papers

You need to review all the previous papers to gain an understanding of the questions. This will give you an idea of the main sections and repetitive questions. Further evaluation of each question is recommended as doing so will guide your study habits towards the concepts and topics on which the questions are based. Apart from this, solving previous papers will also give you an idea of your preparation.

When you practise previous years' question papers, you will know which topics you should study deeply. You will also get to know about the topics that are less important. You should try to solve question papers of at least the last ten years to understand the paper pattern. This will also help you to improve your time-management skills.

Study NCERT Books

The National Council of Educational Research and Training (NCERT) is an independent agency with a mission to provide high-quality education to Indian school children. Although there is a variety of study material available for the UPSC exam, NCERT books are recommended to start with as they discuss the concepts in simple terms. For relevant subjects, students are advised to read NCERT books from Class VI to XII. Since NCERT alone cannot take you ahead, you must ensure that you cover these books as soon as possible. It would be best to finish studying them during the first three months of your preparation.

Practice Test Series

This practice is a crucial part of the last three months of your UPSC exam preparation. Solving mock tests for preliminary and main exams proves beneficial. This helps in two ways. Firstly, you will get a complete idea about the trend of questions asked in the exam. Second, you will be able to manage your time accordingly. According to IAS toppers, these mock tests are an integral part of exam preparation. Practising them regularly will help you improve your speed, assess your preparation, evaluate yourself against your competitors, and boost your confidence.

Need for Modification

Remembering every minute detail of a subject is impossible. Without frequent revision, all your efforts will go in vain and be futile. So, it is necessary to take some time for revision. You can revise all the topics in the weekend to remember them for a long time. Remember that just being a bookworm will not help you clear the exam. Apart from completing the syllabus, your focus should also be on continuously gathering information, developing insight, preparing strategically, revising, practising, and being positive.

Selection of Age

As per UPSC data, the age of candidates who clear the UPSC is 22 years to 28 years. So, preparing for the IAS after the 10th class is too early. You should prepare for the UPSC after the 12th Class. The final year of your graduation is the perfect time to prepare for the UPSC.

Course Checklist

UPSC has made the syllabus of the Civil Services Examination available on its official portal. Keep studying the Civil Services Prelims Syllabus as per your checklist. Once you cover a topic, mark it on the sheet. Use this as an exercise for each topic. Also, you should cover the syllabus extensively and solve each and every topic thoroughly.

UPSC Syllabus Preparation in the Shortest Possible Time

In today's busy life, everyone complains about the lack of time. Those preparing for the UPSC exam also look for ways to complete their syllabus in as limited time as possible. However, it is also true that the syllabus is so vast that it usually takes two years to complete it. Still, with smart work and proper time management, you can complete it in much less than two years.

Preparation should be done by dividing the UPSC exam syllabus into two parts. The first part is the preliminary examination. It consists of two papers – GS (General Studies) and C-SAT. The second part is the main examination and interview. Remember whether it is a preliminary exam or main exam or even the interview, you should not expect the cut-off marks to be less. The result of the examination also proves these facts. So, it would be better for you not to be lax or easy going in your preparation in any way. Prepare your syllabus diligently so that you can perform better than others.

First, go through the conceptual topics which are the five core subjects that you have selected. Along with this, start evaluating yourself for CSAT as well. For this, you should assess and evaluate yourself by solving the previous year's question papers. If you can score up to 100 marks in this, then you do not need to prepare for this part separately. Invest your time in other subjects.

Many aspirants try to study from new sources. But for that, first, the authenticity of those sources should also be checked whether the subject matter that they contain is compatible with the questions appearing in the exam. Along with this, keep track of how many chapters and pages you read per day. Focus on core topics as core topics are good for working professionals, too. After this, your preparation for Basic Science and Tech and Current Affairs continues simultaneously. You can study Ethics even after the preliminary examination.

After covering the syllabus, practise mock tests. But a reasonable limit should be set for solving mock tests, too as too many tests will drain your valuable energy and a smaller number of tests will not prepare you for the exam. Analysing the results after taking the mock tests is an essential exercise. One should not get excited by good performance and dejected by poor performance. You should just try to improve yourself continuously.

Current Affairs plays a significant role in this exam. Read newspapers daily for the preparation of current affairs. Also, read weekly and monthly current affairs online or with the help of a book. Apart from monthly magazines, any half-yearly magazine can also be read for the current affairs of the last six months. You should read newspapers for a maximum of 45 minutes per day; you should not spend more time than this.

Previous year's question papers should be like a radar for preparation giving direction to your preparation. Apart from enhancing your basic knowledge, the previous year's papers also help in developing your mental attitude. They enhance your general knowledge.

Make sure to make notes while studying. That will make it easier for you to revise. It is observed that if we prepare notes in our own way and then read them again, we tend to remember all the facts very quickly. Notes should not be very heavy as the purpose of notes is to cover the important facts of the chapter that you have studied and through them to revise the whole chapter at the time of examination. You can also do this under the guidance of any coaching class.

Now the most important thing - spend your time very wisely. Remember, you are like a person who is short of money and has to spend that money sensibly and economically to grow his business.

Knowledge of the Current Situation

When you prepare for UPSC, you need to have knowledge of every field. It is very important to have knowledge of current affairs because current affairs play a seminal role in the UPSC exam. So, every candidate should make a habit of reading the newspaper daily. You should also make it a habit to pay attention to important things. UPSC Prelims consist of a large number of questions based on current affairs.

Negative Marking

Candidates should note that there is a negative marking of one-third of the marks for each wrong answer in the preliminary examination. The preliminary examination is an elimination test. If you do not limit your negative marks, you will be eliminated from the competition. You should pay attention not to mark wrong answers. Solving mock tests will help you limit your negative marks.

Strategy to Crack UPSC Exam on the First Attempt

You must have read the success stories of many IAS/IPS officers who were able to crack the exam on their very first attempt. Actually, hard work also needs the right direction. If you work hard in the right direction, nothing can stop you from passing the IAS exam.

The UPSC exam can also be cleared with self-study. There are many candidates who are unable to join IAS/IPS coaching classes for various reasons and so prepare for the exam on their own. If you too have decided to do public service by becoming an IAS/IPS officer, then draw your own special strategy.

Syllabus Checklist

Prepare a checklist of the UPSC exam syllabus. Whichever topic you complete, you should keep marking it on the list. You should keep completing the syllabus as per your checklist. You should remember that no subject should be missed.

Strengthen your foundation - Your background does not matter. You just need to understand the basics of the main topics of the UPSC syllabus. So, refer to Class 10-12 NCERT books; they can also be downloaded free of charge from the official website of NCERT. Read them at least twice before making notes.

There is no need to collect too many books for UPSC preparation. Read only specific books, you can also read material on the internet. Apart from this, practise writing more. Before the preliminary exam, complete the main exam syllabus. After that, you should focus the preliminary exam two to three months before it commences. During this, take several mock tests continuously. Many successful IAS/IPS officers also advise candidates to take mock tests to understand their level of preparation. According to them, a mock test is necessary even before the interview.

Set the timings in the day for all the subjects and keep covering the topics accordingly. You must read newspapers every morning for 45 minutes. Current affairs are very important for civil service. You should pay attention to the news along with books every day. Try not to miss even a day's study. Keep studying according to the syllabus daily.

Along with studying, revision is very important for the exam. Try to revise the topics which you have completed every day on the next day. During that time, keep making notes as well.

You should make a timetable for yourself in such a way that you can concentrate on your studies as much as possible and don't waste time on peripheral matters. Whatever happens, you should spend the time you have fixed for studies studying alone. Do not let your mind be diverted by anything else at that time.

Goals are very important in life. You should also make it your goal to clear the UPSC. Whenever you study, don't think that you have to study for 4 hours or 5 hours. Rather decide that today I will get up only after finishing this topic. You should make your goal your dream and you should have the passion to achieve it. Only then you will be able to clear this exam because your colleagues or your rivals will also be preparing in the same way. Your competitors will be more in numbers and selected seats in the exam will be fewer.

Candidates preparing for the UPSC should evolve their own strategy. Then you will be able to prepare according to your ability. There will be many people who will discourage you. In such a scenario, it is necessary to keep yourself positive and keep preparing continuously. Instead of getting nervous and disappointed with failure, review your strategy, and then be willing to make necessary changes.

Success Stories: Hard Work, Patience, Study, Confidence, Courage

Imagine when becoming an IAS officer is so difficult, how difficult it must be to be an IAS topper? After all, what are those special aspects that make someone the topper of this exam? Everyone knows Tina Dabi, who came into the limelight by becoming the topper of IAS-2015 in her first attempt.

To crack this exam, she stresses some important factors—patience, diligence, and discipline, one should never give up, one should never lose hope and one should believe in oneself. Tina loves to study and used to study for 10-12 hours daily to prepare for this exam, which means that the most important element for success in the civil services exam is hard work. So, you should understand one thing - there is no shortcut to succeed in this exam. The harder you work, the more likely you are to be successful.

Ira Singhal, IAS topper of the 2014 batch, gives the mantra of success in this exam and says- "Prepare for this exam, but don't expect anything. Give your best. The most important thing is to prepare the entire syllabus so that no question in the exam comes as a surprise or you should not feel that you have not studied it." Ira says she is an avid reader, especially of novels. She says that she has a collection of 750 novels which she would definitely read someday. This hobby of hers came in handy during her IAS preparation.

To succeed in the IAS, Ira also advises that the most important thing to prepare for this exam is to know about your own weaknesses and strengths and overcome them and prepare accordingly. That's why she cautions against comparing oneself with anyone else. She says - Don't compare yourself with others because everyone's abilities are different. Don't think that if someone studies for 15 hours, then you should also do the same. Prepare according to your ability. In this era of technology, Ira also emphasizes the role of the internet in preparing for this exam.

Gaurav Agarwal, IAS topper of the 2013 batch, says that it is important to learn from mistakes. If you fail in one or two attempts analyse your shortcomings and try to overcome them so that you do not repeat the same mistake again and again. To avoid distractions while preparing for this exam, Gaurav emphasizes the power of self-belief. Acknowledging the power of the internet in today's time, Gaurav says- "Now along with books, the internet also helps appreciably for IAS preparation."

Haritha Kumar, the IAS topper of the 2012 batch, was successful in her fourth attempt. She says that it is clear from her example that one should not give up despite failure. According to her, time management is very important for the preparation for this exam. She is very fond of reading Malayalam and English books. She also reads poems and stories. She says that if you are prepared to work hard, then the entire universe also helps you.

IAS topper of the 2011 batch Shena Agarwal says that those preparing for this exam should remain in solitude. She says that she rectified the mistakes made in her previous attempts and fulfilled her dream of becoming an IAS officer.

As per these toppers, the common factors behind their success are hard work, patience, love for study, self-belief, a never-give-up attitude, learning from mistakes, and preparing the entire syllabus.

These people are not super extraordinary students. It is their passion for their goal that makes them successful. And that is the formula for success.

❑

6

Keeping Your Mind Active

Just like our body, our mind also needs to be healthy in order to function optimally. For this, there are some tips that will not only make your mind work at a faster pace but will also make it easier to remember any lesson for the exam.

Prepare yourself for a brain workout. Mental exercise is different from physical exercise. Chess was invented in our country because it is the most difficult and vigorous exercise for the mind. Of course, not everyone plays chess, but almost everyone likes crossword puzzles or the computer game solitaire. You can start with these. If you don't want to do that either, then the easy exercise is multiplication-division or addition-subtraction.

You should try to memorize a poem or a joke once a week. This will keep your mind balanced and its strength will also increase. You should always think of doing something new. Let new ideas come to the fore. For this, you can think like a child because children think with positive energy, wonder, and curiosity.

Allow yourself to daydream. This will make the brain sharp and its strength will also increase. Do not remain just one person, but create multiple personalities in one person. Think in as many ways as you can.

Is clearing the UPSC Your Dream or Your Need?

You are preparing for UPSC, but have you ever asked yourself a question that why you want to become an IAS/IPS officer? Listen to the question again, why do you want to become an IAS/IPS officer? If the answer to this question is not yet clear to you, then perhaps you are diving into an ocean and you do not know how to reach its shores. So once again ask yourself - why do I want to become an IAS/IPS officer?

The time of exam preparation is a challenging period for the candidates. Due to the vast syllabus and tough competition of this exam, lakhs of candidates fail in the preliminary level exam itself. Do you also want to be one of those who give up on their dreams halfway? Or do you want to be known as a civil servant in your life?

If you want to reach the top, you'll have to do your best and keep in mind that reaching the top is no easy task because the higher you go, the more difficult the journey becomes. So, you have to mould yourself into a superior personality and as a civil service aspirant, move forward to fulfil this mission of becoming an IAS/IPS officer.

If your goal is to succeed in an exam like UPSC, then it is essential that you remove all kinds of fear from your mind. Fear holds you back from doing many things in life. Fear stops you from dreaming about civil services. Many people do not even think of attempting the IAS/IPS exam. Remember, "this fear is only a mental state" which can be overcome by faultless preparation and skilful practice. So, prepare for the UPSC exam with courage and enthusiasm, and also keep testing and practising continuously for your personal development. Also, remember that in the UPSC interview, your personality and your balanced thinking is the key to your success.

Once you overcome the fear, it is then time to increase your confidence. Determination and will power has the magic power to take you to any height of success. You should stick to your determination to become an IAS/IPS officer. Do not have any kind of confusion or doubt. For the development of your knowledge, you require help from other sources, too. Therefore, be guided by your seniors and experts.

You should remember the saying - "No Pain, No Gain", that is, no success is possible without hard work and dedication. To be successful, you have to step out of your comfort zone and take the necessary steps for your own welfare. Instead of complaining about what you do not have, you should always be thankful to God for what you have now. If you have a healthy mind and body, you will definitely be able to clear this exam. All you need is the right attitude and confidence. So, always remain positive and principled.

An English film named Apollo 13A was released in 1998. There is a dialogue in that movie – "failure is not an option." If you want to qualify for IAS/IPS, then you should make this your motto and always think that no matter what happens, you will not fail. When someone asks you why you are preparing for the UPSC, your answer should be - Because this is the most important thing for me. Success or failure is not in your hands. But if you pursue a goal thinking that apart from it, nothing else is possible, then your perseverance will start paying off automatically.

Can an average student become an IAS/IPS officer?

In our country, the Civil Services Examination is considered so highly prestigious that often on seeing a civil servant, we assume that he must have been a very bright student. There is no doubt that people who qualify for IAS/IPS are very well-informed and hardworking. But you will be surprised to know that most of the people who pass civil service examinations every year were average students during their school days. This means that to qualify for UPSC, it is not necessary for you to have been a meritorious student.

"Successful people don't do different things, they do things differently."

This means that you need not do anything different to be successful, but you should know the art of doing work in a different way. When you understand this theory and implement it, your success story will start immediately. If you have an ordinary academic background or you never topped the class does not mean that you cannot become an IAS/IPS officer. All it takes is a slight change in routine and tremendous discipline. The UPSC syllabus is vast and takes time to complete. If you are planning to prepare for UPSC, first of all, you must assess your time. Read the entire syllabus carefully and understand it and then get an idea of how much time you will need to complete it. Do not overestimate yourself by being overconfident, nor get defeated by the syllabus by being underconfident. Rather make a realistic estimation and prepare a roadmap ahead.

Divide the UPSC syllabus into small parts and focus on each part. Set small goals for yourself because they will help you achieve your biggest goals. Undoubtedly, the UPSC syllabus is quite vast, but if you follow the strategy of "divide and conquer", you can easily crack it.

Everyone studies. But what is important is how well you can write what you have studied. For this, answer writing practice is necessary. So, take many mock tests. But do this only after preparing for the preliminary exam. Till you do not remember the facts, what will you write in the main exam answers and by whom will you get them checked? So, after preparing for the preliminary exam, write the answers for the main exam. First, write only a few answers and after some practice, solve the entire paper. Go through the previous year's papers, take mock tests, and write down the answers to see if there are any gaps. If you find any shortcomings, you should remove them immediately.

Take responsibility for fulfilling your purpose and avoid the tendency to procrastinate. You should always remember that successful people are in control of themselves and believe that only they are responsible for their results. So, use the timetable to organize yourself for a day, a week, and a month for exam preparation. Instead of putting off or delaying the topic which you find most difficult during preparation, try to study that first and have strong determination.

8 Myths Related to the UPSC Exam

The post of IAS/IPS is prestigious and the myths associated with it are equally big. If you are preparing for IAS, then you must have surely heard a few things related to it. Many people continue believing these things even after preparing for years and somehow it affects their preparation as well. But there is no need to worry. The 8 myths related to UPSC are as follows –

1. **The UPSC exam is the toughest exam** – This myth seems to be true because the success rate of the exam is very low. But the truth is that out of lakhs of candidates who apply for the exam, only half appear for this exam, and then out of that only 20% make serious preparation and take the exam. However, it is also true that if you keep practising continuously, then you can be easily successful in this exam.

2. **It is necessary to study for 16-18 hours daily** – Many people must have advised you that it is necessary to study for 15 – 16 hours every day to clear the UPSC exam. There is no doubt that the civil services exam requires a lot of time for studying. But to say that it is necessary to study 16-18 hours a day to crack this exam is not entirely correct. Your success depends on factors other than hours of study. It is natural that the abilities of the candidates will be different. Some candidates may understand a subject quickly and some may take a while. Apart from this, if a candidate studies regularly for 8 hours under efficient guidance, then his chances of success increase.

3. **Only academic toppers can clear the IAS/IPS exam** - It is believed that only academic toppers can clear this exam. But every year, the list of IAS/IPS toppers seems to bust

this myth. Many toppers come from nondescript schools and colleges and many come from backward areas of the country with practically no scope for any kind of guidance. Many toppers are also average academic performers.

4. **One must know everything to become an IAS/IPS officer-** Another myth about the exam is that students appearing for the exam must know everything. The syllabus is certainly vast. But the fact is that it is also well-defined. The Current Affairs topic can be somewhat broad, but that too can be covered with the right strategy. So, the truth is that following the syllabus is the right way to crack the exam.

5. **Luck is necessary to pass this exam** - A general belief among the students preparing for this exam is that luck is necessary to clear this exam. If you believe in luck, then you must clearly understand that your luck contributes only 1 per cent and your hard work contributes 99 per cent to pass the exam. Don't let the 99 per cent of success slip through your hands. If you work sincerely, luck will certainly favour you.

6. **Candidates should read as many books as possible** - IAS/IPS aspirants should read many books. But they are not advised to collect as many books on one subject as possible and try to read them all. They should read the best books on each subject.

7. **It is impossible to crack the IAS/IPS exam without coaching** - There is also a common belief that without coaching it is impossible to crack the IAS/IPS exam. This is just a myth. In today's times, it is no longer necessary for students to attend coaching classes. Everything is available at the click of a button. The candidates can get the best notes for UPSC exam-related current affairs magazines, RSTV programmes, etc. online and mostly free of cost on the Internet.

8. **Candidates from the English medium score more marks as compared to the Hindi medium -** It is said that the English medium candidates score more marks in the examination as compared to those from the Hindi medium. This too is a myth. Getting good marks in a subject depends on the candidate's interest in that subject, his comprehensive understanding, availability of standard study material, acceptable writing style and time management. The candidate should choose the subject in which he/she is comfortable as an optional subject.

Overcome the Fear of Exam

Many students feel anxious just thinking about the exam. They start thinking, 'Will I be able to answer all the questions?', 'It would have been better if I had studied a little more.' etc. These thoughts bother almost every student. A slight amount of stress helps in better performance. It releases adrenaline hormones in the body, which keeps the person alert and focused.

It is natural to have some tension or pressure, but excessive nervousness causes problems. It surrounds the person with negativity and then he is unable to concentrate and think. This has a negative effect on performance as the student is neither able to concentrate on the questions nor is able to give accurate answers. There are many ways by which the fear of examination can be overcome so that the students can offer their best.

Before the Exam Complete your syllabus well in time and revise it at least a day in advance. Studying till the last moment increases stress. There can be different ways in which the mind can be kept stable and calm. Some people find listening to music relaxing while others find exercising relaxing. Bathing with lukewarm water can also be an effective way to relax. Choose your own way of relaxation.

Such measures can be very beneficial on the day of the examination and the day before that. They help in remembering whatever you have studied and also boost your confidence. Not knowing the way to the exam centre can also lead to anxiety. You should collect information about it in advance and if possible, you should go there once and see it yourself. This will save you from last minute rush. Read the rules of the examination carefully. Be sure to get enough sleep the night before the exam.

During the Exam

If you haven't studied, then the thought "I don't know anything." can disturb you; but getting such thoughts even after studying well is a sign of nervousness. Students are unable to concentrate due to stress. Some cannot even read the question properly. To avoid this, you can take the following measures –

- Reach the examination hall on time. After reaching the hall, take long deep breaths and exhale. People often cannot breathe properly when they are in panic mode. Take deep breaths and straighten your back.
- Try to concentrate by looking at a still, inanimate object (wall, picture, etc.) in front of you.
- Repeat something positive in your mind, like - I am going to pass this exam. Keep repeating this for 1-2 minutes and then breathe normally. You will feel relaxed.
- Read the questions carefully. If you start feeling nervous again in the middle of the exam, repeat the concentration exercises.
- Decide the strategy to solve the question paper, e.g., which questions you would solve first, etc., and start writing the answers without wasting time.

Ways to Increase Memory

When it comes to remembering anything, the mind takes decisions on the basis of the meaning, value, and appropriateness of that thing. The mind also sets priorities in this order. The first step to remembering is knowing the meaning. So, to remember anything, you should first understand its essential meaning.

If you do not understand the meaning, then there is no point in rote learning. Therefore, first understand the meaning of the topic or lesson that has to be remembered, then understand its importance and value. After this, know what is the appropriateness of that subject in your life.

Success Story: The Journey from Labourer to IAS

One day, a child was working as a labourer at a famine relief site, when some officials came there for an investigation. He learnt that they would give their report to the highest authority, i.e., Collector. On that day he decided that he wanted to become a collector.

This might seem like an inconsequential story, but it is a very inspiring account of the struggle of 30-year-old Hukmaram Chowdhary, who secured 110th rank in the Union Public Service Commission examination. He is the first IAS officer from his village. Hukmaram, a resident of Bherunda, a small village in Nagaur, says that his father was an asthma patient. So, he had to shoulder the responsibility of the family since childhood.

Along with going to school, Hukmaram worked in the farm and also as a labourer during the summer holidays. He did not give up even in adverse circumstances. After passing his 12th Class examination, he completed his graduation and started giving tuitions to the children in the village. After that he completed his M.Sc.

By the time he had graduated, Hukmaram was selected through the teacher recruitment exam, but his aim was to become an IAS officer. He stayed in Delhi for a whole year and prepared for the exam. His hard work paid off. When the villagers got the news of his becoming an IAS officer, the entire village took out a procession in his honour.

Hukmaram says, "It is necessary to work sincerely to achieve the goal." Hukmaram has set an example for the youth. No matter how difficult the path to the destination is, one has to work conscientously to reach it.

❑

7

Develop Common Successful Habits

If you want to be successful in the IAS/IPS exam, then adopt the habits of successful people in your life.

Only Believe in Winning

Successful people never give up; they only believe in winning. It is not as if they do not face difficulties in their life or they never experience failure. Everyone faces difficult situations in their lives. Everyone has to face failure in life. But successful people don't stop there; instead, they move ahead faster.

Focus on Work

Successful people simply focus on their work. They don't care about what the world is doing. People who win don't care about what their opponents are doing. World famous investor Warren Buffett says, "Let people focus on their competitors, we just have to focus on our business." It is clear from this that successful people think only about their victory. Successful people know that their goal is a significant part of their lives.

Planning Work

All successful people plan their work, see the positive and negative points in their work, set a time frame to achieve their goal, and think about what they have to do for that and how many hours they have to work for that. They then work accordingly towards their goal every day. But common people do not have any plans. They start working from any point and they do not have any purpose. That's why they are not successful.

Do Everything Well

Some people try to give their best in everything they do, be it a big or small job. This habit takes them to the pinnacle of success. Whenever you do any work, try your best to give your 100 per cent to it. You should remember that nothing is achieved without hard work. So, you should avoid shortcuts and work hard.

Always Learning Something New

A successful person always keeps alive the desire to learn something new, e.g., a new sport, a new cuisine, or even a new language. His habit of learning something new every day helps him to be different from and more successful than other people. If you also want to be successful, keep the desire to learn continuously alive in you.

Strong Will Power

Successful people have strong will power and they are determined. That is why nothing is impossible for them. With their strong will, they make everything possible. This habit takes them ahead in life. If you have undertaken a task, then do not back down even if you face failure. Display your strong determination and remain engaged in it giving it your all till you are successful.

Positive Thinking

All the successful people and achievers in the world always keep their thinking positive. They undertake every task with positive thinking because your thinking determines the result of your work.

Successful people always have positive thinking. They never focus on problems. Rather, whenever they get an opportunity, they try with positive energy, due to which they get quick success.

The formula to be successful is - "Always keep your attitude positive." A great person once said that you become what you think because your thought creates you.

Being Proactive

Being proactive means being aware of oneself. Confidence and self-awareness is the definition of being proactive. A proactive person understands his responsibility well and does not blame circumstances for his behaviour.

That means active people are those who set their goals according to their will. No person or problem can distract such people from their goals and objectives because such people do not let others control them, rather they are in control of themselves.

Starting Work with the End in Mind

Starting with the end in mind means that before starting any work, you have a firm idea of its end. Those who are sure of the end, do their work with full dedication; no matter how many obstacles they encounter, they do not back down. They are well aware of the result of their work. Starting a journey with a clear understanding of your destination means knowing where you are going. If you are well aware of where you are at present, then only will you take the future steps in the right direction.

Focus on the Set Target

All the great people in the world in the past or all the great and successful people in the present focus fully on the goal they set for themselves. Successful people do not base their goals on someone else's success or on someone else's insistence. Rather they have their own desire to achieve a goal. Every successful person has some or other goal in life and he works hard day and night to achieve his goal. Successful people do not change their goals on account of minor difficulties, rather they learn from them.

Learning Continuously

Learning is something that helps you become successful in anything. Successful people know this very well. That's why they believe in continuous learning. By learning you can achieve any goal in the world. Elon Musk who is a big revolutionary did not know anything about rocket science nor did he formally study rocket science. Nevertheless, he read books and made a rocket and became the richest person in the world. This shows that if a person believes in learning, then he can achieve every goal.

Punctuality

There is a saying that the person who does not respect time, time does not respect him. If money is lost, one can earn it again. But the time that has elapsed does not return. Successful people respect the time and they sleep on time and wake up on time. No one can stop those who are punctual from reaching the heights of success. Hence whatever you do in life, you should be punctual.

Thinking About Unimportant People

Don't waste time thinking about those who will not lead you to any progress or achievement in your work. Your family or friends are the only people you really need to think about. Often, people start thinking about some actor, actress or any other person to whom they do not have access.

Checking Phone

People are frequently seen checking their phones continuously during conversations, which is a very annoying habit. Do not look at your phone repeatedly while talking to someone. Do not even reply to messages during that time. Although the person in front of you will not react when you do such things, they will certainly not appreciate your behaviour and it will also have an adverse effect on your conversation.

Checking mail while working

Checking phone messages or emails in the middle of work is also a habit that adversely affects your efficiency. You shouldn't be in a rush to check every message, popup, tweet, or email right away. You should pay full attention to the work you are doing. Once you finish it, check the message or email again.

Waiting for Good Work to Come Along

Thinking that you should wait to do some work till you feel that you will be successful is wrong because you cannot say that you will be successful at the start of any work. That's why you should start the work. Whether you succeed or fail comes later.

Speaking Ill of Someone

Speaking ill of someone tarnishes your image. It is better to spend your time in creative pursuits or work. This will not only lead to progress in your work but will also earn you respect from others.

Learning to Say 'No'

Sometimes it is difficult to say no to a friend or colleague, but there is no harm in saying no. Most people will understand and you don't need to think too much about those who won't. When you say no, you will feel bad for a while. But if you say yes, you may feel even worse for a long time.

Success Story: There Must Be a Fire Inside You

Divya, who is a 2015 batch IAS officer, says, "To crack the civil services exam, you need to have a fire inside you. You have to find your own reason why you want to pass this exam. This same reason is what helps you sail through tough times."

While preparing for the Civil Services Examination, the following thoughts must have surely arisen in your mind –

- I am tired of the preparation.
- I am feeling cut off from the world.
- I could not get enough time to prepare.
- I feel like giving it up.

If your answer is yes, then IAS officer Divya Loganathan from the 2015 batch can guide you. Her All-India rank in the IAS exam was 402 and she stepped into a prestigious field of the fourth pillar of democracy. But her journey was not easy either. She faced challenges and also failed twice in the IAS exam.

Find the Fire Inside You

Divya says you must have a fire inside you to crack the Civil Services Exam. She says that you have to find the reason why you want to clear this exam. That same reason will help you in difficult times as well.

After successfully passing the exam, Divya says, "I took myself very seriously during my preparation. This exam was like a sword around my neck. You should enjoy the entire UPSC journey just as you celebrate your success."

Make a Time Table and Follow It

Whether you study for 10 hours a day or 4 hours a day, it is very important to make a timetable before starting the preparation for the Civil Services Exam. This not only inculcates discipline in you but also helps you to prepare with full commitment. Along with this, it guards you against bad habits. That's why a time table is necessary to achieve your goal in a specified time.

Study In Small Slots

Divya says, "If you think that you will practise after completing the syllabus, then your strategy is totally wrong. Preparation and practice should go hand-in-hand. Practising again and again is the only way to succeed in this exam. I would advise all the students preparing for the competitive exams to practise answer writing on a daily basis."

She says that for this, the contestants need to spare some time every day. She advises them to make time slots for all the subjects, which can be completed easily. For example, they could practise two questions every day after lunch or two questions in the evening. She says, "Make it a habit. You'll see how easy it becomes in the end."

Take Out Some Time for Yourself

Divya says that every contestant should also take some time out for themselves during their preparation. Recalling her preparation days, she says, "I never took out time to watch a film. I wish I had watched films, too! I now realize how watching a good film can change a person's outlook."

She encourages the aspirants to watch films. Movies not only present the world view but also make us ambitious. She says, "You would be surprised as to how much you can learn by watching stimulating thought-provoking movies and how much they make a lasting impression on you. Movies can both stimulate or inspire you and provide relief."

Using Online Educational Tools

Divya says, "E-learning tools have developed a lot and everyone should use them. The biggest advantage of these online tools is that you can access them from anywhere. But it is important to remember that one must not get caught up in the internet. Time is critical during UPSC preparation. So, find a useful website and go through its material repeatedly. Don't waste your time searching for a new website every day."

Make Effective Notes

"While making notes during preparation, you must ensure that they are not too long. Try to cover the notes of each chapter in a maximum of two or three pages, only then they will be useful. There is no point in going through several pages of notes during revision.

Divya says, "Revision is as important as preparation. So, I made notes in such a way that I had a strong hold on them."

Build Your Own Path

"Before you start the preparation, it is imperative for you to understand that every competitor has to decide his/her own journey. There is no point in comparing yourself with others. Although it is not easy to control your mind you should not get upset by comparing yourself with others. If you believe in yourself and work hard, everything will turn out well for you."

Divya says, "Remember that every competitor has their own struggle. So, taking inspiration is a different thing, but there is no use in making comparisons. I used to be very depressed at times and I used to think how difficult life is and it affected me negatively. So, you should think positively, move ahead and reach your destination."

Do Not Be Afraid, Be Brave

It is natural to feel pressure when the exam approaches. But you should not panic, you should be brave, and just focus on what you want to achieve.

Face the test with a positive mindset. Even after clearing the exam, you should not think that you have reached your destination. In fact, this is just the beginning and there are many more challenges and disappointments to be faced. So, be in control of yourself.

❑

8

IAS/IPS Exams: Creating Your Own Strategy

Your strategy is the most important thing for success in the civil services exam. You cannot pass this exam with the help of others. Only your confidence, will power, and instinct can lead you to success. If you follow a great motivation for success in this service, then it will definitely help you. This motivation can be about social service, proving oneself to the society or winning someone's heart.

In a notebook, note down whatever information you get about civil services from newspapers or from interviews of successful people. Information should be relevant.

Choose your optional subject very carefully keeping in mind the points such as your interest, availability of study material, nature of questions, scoring, etc. You may take suggestions from everyone, but you must make your own decisions. Always remember that the subject is not important, what is important is your hold on it and your success.

You should make a strategy for each part of the preliminary and main exam and see what your strengths and weaknesses are. Build a strategy by focusing on your strengths and gradually reducing your weaknesses while trying to convert them into your strengths.

You have to score at least 225 marks in the optional subject and at least 75 marks in General Studies. A target of 300 is quite reasonable for prelims. By setting goals in this manner, you can achieve them.

Prepare for the essay from the very beginning. You can prepare many topics of general studies which are related to social issues in the form of an essay.

While preparing, your entire focus should be on the main exam. For the preliminary exam, 6 months prior to the exam is sufficient. Also, you can make necessary changes according to your need. But please keep in mind that before the preliminary exam, you have carried out preparations for the main exam once. This will boost your confidence.

How to prepare yourself to become an IAS/IPS officer?

If I ask you why it is so difficult to become an IAS officer, what would be your answer? Is it because of the vast syllabus or because of only a slight chance of success? Or is it because of its pattern? All these answers are correct to some extent, but the accurate answer is lifestyle. You may find it somewhat strange. But it is absolutely true that becoming an IAS/IPS officer is difficult because most people cannot adopt the lifestyle it requires, due to which they are not able to cross the other hurdles of this exam.

Knowledge needed for becoming an IAS/IPS officer can be obtained from books and other resources, but we cannot get information about other factors like lifestyle qualities such as self-discipline, motivation, and punctuality from books. Human beings develop these qualities within themselves and for this, it is necessary to change some of their habits. Today we will learn about some such habits.

Developing the Habit of Reading

The only way to cover the ever-expanding syllabus of the CSAT exam and even the extensive syllabus of subject-specific papers is by developing the habit of reading. This habit of reading cannot be forced upon you, it should happen naturally. So, if you are preparing for the IAS/IPS exam, then being a bookworm will definitely work in your favour. Apart from this, you should also try to read different types of books. Include a variety and wide range of books in your reading schedule and diversify your reading habits.

Proper use of the Internet

In today's time, with the help of an effective medium like the Internet you can get whatever information you want. However, you have to use it properly. Otherwise, you are at risk of becoming addicted to it and then you would end up wasting your valuable time. Most candidates do not realize that government websites are a simple, accessible source of policies, plans, programmes, data, and reports. The information you will get and the understanding you will develop by studying these websites will be beneficial for both preliminary and the main examination. Also, apart from websites specially made for IAS/IPS aspirants, you can also use YouTube, Google News, Wikipedia, and other such websites or alternative sources.

Problem-Solving Attitude

You will need problem-solving skills not only to crack the exam but also while working as an IAS/IPS officer. You will be confronted with many challenges and you will have to deal with them with new technologies. You may have to face challenges like extensive syllabus, time management, proper/inappropriate resources, pressure from society, etc. In such situations, your problem-solving attitude will come in handy and prove useful.

Be your own teacher

Preparing for the UPSC is a long and exhausting task. It seems as if its syllabus is ever expanding. In such a situation, depending on any one teacher/guide/mentor or material from any one coaching class will not work. You have to be your own teacher. So, frame your own questions and find the answers using your reference and study materials. Playing the role of both teacher and student will instil confidence in you that will carry you through the exam and beyond.

Commitment and Dedication

The path to success in the UPSC is a long and difficult one. Only your commitment will help you in completing this journey. You will come across many challenges and problems and your resolve may waver. Despite all the challenges, it is also true that every year some candidates crack this exam with the help of their determination. For this, it is necessary that you have faith in yourself and a spirit of dedication towards your goal.

When should the first attempt for IAS/IPS be made?

Civil Services Examination is an open field where everyone has the right to make an effort. Many youths of our country dream of becoming IAS/IPS and try their luck, but very few people are successful. Do you know the reason? Because they appear in this exam either without preparation or with incomplete preparation. To reduce the crowd, the UPSC has fixed the number of attempts for each candidate. So, those who take the exam without preparation waste one attempt after another, while some candidates appear for the exam recognizing the seriousness of the first attempt. But how does one decide when one should make the first attempt?

You should take the decision of joining the civil services after the 12th standard. It takes at least 2 to 3 years to prepare for civil services. So, you should start preparing for it during graduation itself. You should start your preparation with NCERT books. Along with this, you should keep the complete syllabus of the Civil Services Examination with you and prepare accordingly.

Most of the candidates choose a subject from graduation as an optional subject for the main examination. This makes it easy for you as you study this subject for three whole years during graduation. Apart from this, for other selected optional subjects, you can choose study material or seek expert advice.

Now the question is what you should do during these two-three years so that you will be fully prepared for your first attempt.

Before starting the preparation, you need to prepare yourself mentally and physically for the exam. You should set goals and devote time effectually. You should set a comfortable, but fixed time table before your preparation and stick to it. Making a time table will make your preparation easier and more organized. With the time limit, you will be able to work better and complete the syllabus faster.

You must understand and follow the syllabus of the Civil Services Examination. Knowing the syllabus will help you choose relevant study material, prioritize topics, etc.

You can use your time in college to gain knowledge of various subjects by engaging in deep discussions on various issues with students from other disciplines. University is an excellent place to hone writing and communication skills where you can participate in various activities like essay writing competitions, debates, working for the university magazine, or joining NSS.

You should read NCERT books. You should read them at least twice before reading any other book. You should also prepare your own notes which will help you in revision as the exam approaches.

You should prepare for the preliminary exam and mains exam together. That means you should practise answer-writing along with studying. Of course, when the exam is near, you may prepare only for the preliminary exam.

Practising mock tests before the exam will also benefit you. The more you practise at home, the more comfortable you will be in the exam hall.

While you all this, two years will have passed and by then your preparation would be complete. So, before your first attempt, you should make serious efforts for at least two years.

Selection of Optional Subject

Some subjects can be selected because they help in scoring high marks and general studies and essay can be selected due to maximum representation, such as Geography, Political Science, Public Administration, History, and Sociology - which are easy and also prove helpful in General Studies question papers. In particular, there are 30-35 questions from Geography in the preliminary examination, whereas in the main examination, questions worth 120 marks each from Geography, History, and Political Science appeared. Most of the questions in essay writing have appeared from Sociology, Geography, History, and Economy.

Choice of Medium

There is no discrimination in the Civil Services Examination on the basis of language. Therefore, aspirants can find success equally through both English and Hindi mediums. But the reason for the low percentage of success in Hindi medium is the lack of study material and whatever is available is unauthentic and superficial. Model questions and answers of the Civil Services Exam are based on standard English books and so, Hindi medium students have to study those books, too.

Importance of Science as a Subject

The prevalence of science subjects in the civil service exam is continuously decreasing. The reason for this is the vast syllabus and the complexity of the subjects. Science students should choose such subjects in which the basic principle of science is used, but the content is practical and related to the common life, e.g., geography, which combines science and art.

Preparation for the Interview

There is a misconception about the interview that it is a test of candidates' knowledge, whereas, in reality, it is a personality assessment, in which your efficiency and ethical skills are tested. Through the interview, the psychology of the candidates and their sensitivity towards current events, and their ability to take prudent decisions are also tested. During the interview, nationalist thoughts should be expressed in place of narrow parochial thoughts like regionalism.

Have Control Over Time

Time management is very important in the preparation for any exam. Preparing for nine question papers in such a short time is not easy. But it can be well managed with time management. Candidates can adopt time management practices according to their ability. You should make sure to devote at least ten hours of study time daily to the main examination. As the subject is vast, you should set aside four hours daily for general studies.

Writing Practice

Many times, it happens that despite knowing the answer to a question, you are not able to write it. There are two reasons for this - lagging behind in writing speed or lack of time management in answering the question. Lagging behind in writing means you are not able to match your writing speed with the available time. To overcome this, you should practise solving the model question papers prepared by yourself or from any book or magazine in the stipulated time. Questions are missed in the exam due to the lack of time management or not following the word limit. Answer the questions accurately, avoiding confusion and disorientation.

Some Unmistakable Habits for Success

To make the answer effective, use the statements and quotes by various authors about the aspects related to the possible questions.

Make a detailed study of the original works of the authors/ writers.

Pay attention to brief notes and explanations.

Try to remain stress-free by managing time.

Pay special attention to the fact that there should be no grammatical errors in the Hindi question paper.

Use your knowledge while maintaining composure when answering questions which you are not comfortable with.

Accuracy should be emphasized. Don't waste time trying to write more metaphorical language.

Practise reading and writing as much as possible to maintain consistency in the flow of language while answering questions.

Take the help of a competent guide to check the correctness and accuracy of questions that you solve for practice.

Special attention should be paid to the chapters that are added after the change made to the syllabus.

In order to maintain balance in positive and negative aspects for the sake of the objectivity of the answer, understand both sides thoroughly.

Keep an eye on current events and pay special attention to aspects related to them.

Pay attention to the constitutional aspects related to administrative work.

To make your writing effective, you should mention the names of the books of the scholars, their principles, and recommendations. A compilation of some principles and scholars can be prepared for this.

While answering the questions in the examination, the evaluation should be your own and not that of the writers or scholars.

Identify the main section by analysing the previous year's questions and also identify the nature of the questions.

Prepare the answer format for all the questions and practise accordingly.

Compile authentic facts correctly because errors in facts will have a negative effect.

Make special preparation for two marks questions and short notes. You get almost 100 per cent marks in them.

While solving model question papers, one should practise writing answers exactly as per the questions.

Develop the writing style in such a way that your answers reflect the mindset and broad liberal thinking of a civil servant.

You should try to add more than one dimension contained in the questions along with fluency in the language. For this, you should read newspapers and magazines regularly and make notes of important facts.

You should properly analyse the previous year's questions and mark the important section or question. It will make it easy to prepare the whole syllabus.

To bring originality to writing, you should pay special attention to getting familiar with the basic spirit of the subject. This will also increase your analytical ability.

Regular practice of writing is very important since the questions are of a descriptive type.

You should keep the answers completely factual. Also, you should keep the answers close to the basic concepts and ideas to avoid the fear of deviation. You should avoid any bias while answering the questions as doing so can prove fatal.

While preparing, keep in mind the important topics and also their importance from the point of view of the exam.

While answering the questions, you should pay special attention to the time limit. Spending more time on one answer will give you less time for other answers.

Marks are not awarded for superficial knowledge in the main exam. So, you should lay emphasis on critical study of all aspects.

Just collecting facts is not enough, you should develop an analytical approach.

You should make short notes of possible and important chapters.

You should practise writing notes as much as possible.

You should lay emphasis on expressing your concept in as simple language as possible.

Questions about maps are also asked under the subject. That's why you should especially prepare for them.

You should interact with subject matter experts; this will bring clarity in answering questions. Practise as many questions as possible asked in previous exams.

Habits for Success

Devotion to the goal, ability to work hard, continuous study for at least a year, correct selection of optional subjects, the study of authentic books, strong hold on current affairs, good language style, making short notes, studying original books for theory, reading newspapers and news, practising the questions that are asked, continuous practice of difficult questions, deep study of

IGNOU books, preparation by making notes, practicing answer writing, focusing on time management, giving equal time to all the questions and keeping an eye on the major events of the country and abroad.

You should prepare according to the syllabus. You should go through the previous year's questions. Prepare for Geography in a scientific way. Read NCERT books to get clarity on concepts. Reading is essential to prepare for conceptually ideological questions. You should pay special attention to questions related to statistics, maps, economic survey and census.

You should practise by preparing a list of physical topographies, geographical structures, cities, etc. through a map. For Geography, the more you practise maps the better will be your score. Instead of reading too many books, read books by selected and important authors.

How to Make Notes

Notes are very important in the preparation of the civil service examination. Good notes play a key role in helping you make a balanced and effective strategy for your preparation. Also, they help you in revising the entire syllabus in a shorter time.

Linear Notes

This method works better for those students who cannot make detailed notes due to lack of time. In this method, important lines or facts (dates, figures, etc.) are underlined with different coloured pens or pencils in the textbook itself. However, this is fine only when the entire matter is well organized. The disadvantage of this method is that time is unnecessarily wasted in searching for the matter during revision as the entire material is scattered. Hence, it is better to make notes in a plain register or on a loose sheet. You should keep half of the page blank, so that you can write facts and information that you will get later.

Pattern Notes

This method is also called 'Skeleton method'. In this method, the subject is divided into different chapters and topics. Then the main points and facts of each topic are written in the form of small points heading wise, pictorial form, etc. Not only are they easy to replicate, but they also take up less of your time. You are able to compare, relate and understand each subject and topic. Such notes are useful like a panacea at the last minute and it becomes easy to understand the whole subject and make a clear strategy.

Can one prepare for the IAS and State Service Examination (PSC) simultaneously?

Although there are many government job opportunities in our country, due to the rising competition every year, the opportunities are also decreasing. In such a scenario, many students decide to prepare for the IAS and PSC together. But is it really possible to prepare for both these exams together?

The answer to this question is 'Yes!' One can prepare for both these exams together as there is a lot of similarity in eligibility, pattern and syllabus for both the exams. For this, it is mandatory for the applicant to have a Bachelor's degree in any discipline from any recognized university. Both PSC and IAS exams have 3 stages-

1. Preliminary Examination
2. Main Examination
3. Interview

When it comes to the syllabus, in PSC, the number of questions related to that particular state is slightly more but they can be broadly covered in the preparation for the IAS.

Now the question is how to prepare for both exams together. Candidates appearing for both IAS Civil Services Exam and State

PSC Exam often feel confused about the right strategy to adopt to prepare for both exams simultaneously. Since the syllabus of both exams is vast and there is a shortage of time for the candidates, it is essential that they should adopt a proper approach to the preparation. Directionless preparation at such times will not give you the desired results.

Before you understand 'how to study', you must answer these important questions - what is your real interest, what is your goal, do you get bored of studying after some time, do you lack confidence, etc? Try to find out - Why is a certain person successful? Is that person special? No. A person is never special, only his style is special. By that, it means that his way of working is special. You too can become like that successful person. You just have to adopt a special way of doing your work.

First of all, make a timetable according to your daily routine. For example, are you preparing for the PSC and IAS as a working person or are a you student? So, if you are a student, then according to the time available to you, you should make a timetable for 8-10 hours of study. If you are preparing for PSC and IAS while working, then you should make a timetable for at least 5-6 hours of study daily.

You can divide one or two topics for a week. You should decide whether you would study them this week. When you feel that the particular topic of a subject has been covered, then solve the questions related to it. Only then should you study the other topics. Before you start another topic, make sure to revise the previously studied topic once.

For current affairs, you must read a newspaper daily, so that you can stay updated with national and international news. Make sure to make notes in a notebook while reading the paper. If you enjoy reading a magazine like *Pratiyogita Darpan, Manthan* etc. - you will find many such magazines in the market - you can buy one of them a month.

When you start feeling bored while studying, you can practise maths and reasoning. Actually, Maths and Reasoning help you get rid of boredom or else you can take a break of 5-10 minutes and do whatever makes you feel refreshed. You can listen to your favourite music or read any current affairs magazine.

You should use only a few selected books while studying. You should try to make point-wise notes in a notebook instead of just highlighting the points in the book while reading the topics because when it is exam time, these notes will prove to be a milestone in your success. If we decide to read heavy books just before the exam, then it can lower our morale and we can lose confidence and become depressed.

Success Story: Drawing Inspiration from Suffering

You can achieve a good rank in the Civil Services Examination in the very first attempt despite living in the midst of poverty. Harish Chandra from Delhi is a living example of this. He achieved 309th rank at the age of 21 and prepared for the exam in the college library, park and lawn.

Harishchandra says, "I grew up in the midst of poverty. My mother raised me while working as a maid in other people's houses and my father worked as a daily wage labourer. As I grew up, I would feel extreme pain seeing the condition of my parents and home. Though I never expected a miracle in my life, my world changed when I joined Hindu College after the 12th standard. In a way, it was the turning point in my life. I found a very congenial environment in Hindu College for studies from the very beginning. This boosted my confidence manifold. That was the time I started thinking of becoming an IAS officer.

Since I used to work in a shop along with my studies till Class 10, my marks were very low as I could not study properly. In Class 12, I gave up the job in the shop and started giving tuition while studying. That helped me a lot and I scored 80 percent marks in Class 12. I got 80 percent marks. Ashu Mishra, who was my classmate in college, made me realize a few things. Earlier, I used to consider myself inferior. But Ashu's spirit inspired me to move forward. Ashu is blind, yet he maintains a positive attitude and moves forward. Inspired by him, I also started pushing myself forward. Additionally, I was also immensely impressed by the success of Govind Jaiswal, the son of a rickshaw puller, and became convinced that even a person without means can become an IAS officer through his efforts. Apart from all this, I received full support from my mother, father, and teacher.

As my financial condition was insecure, I set the target in phases and started working towards achieving it. First of all, I got a firm grasp on my subjects. This increased my confidence. I received a scholarship from the university. So, I did not face much difficulty in studying. With the support of my parents, I was motivated to do something different. First of all, I studied diligently for my BA. I scored 64 per cent marks in the BA. My subjects in BA were Political Science and Philosophy. With these two subjects, I started dreaming of becoming an IAS officer. I was too young to take the Civil Services exam. So, I did my MA and received JRF in the first attempt.

I used to study for eight to ten hours daily for IAS preparation. I started serious preparation a year before the exam. First of all, I went through the previous year's questions and started preparing accordingly. I divided the time subject-wise for the preparation. I read the newspaper every day. That helped me a lot in the preparation of current affairs. I believe that coaching is not necessary to succeed in the Civil Services Examination. Coaching can only give direction. Success comes only through one's own effort. I took guidance from Patanjali IAS Coaching to prepare for Philosophy, as a result of which I could score better.

This was my first attempt. After clearing the preliminary exam, I prepared for the main exam. I did all my studies at home. I would go on walks to keep myself refreshed. I started preparing with the help of question banks and teachers. I didn't face much difficulty in the main exam because I had studied both political science and philosophy during my BA. I did not study too many books. I used NCERT as a foundation. Being an arts student, I faced some difficulties in statistics. But with incessant practice, I was successful in that, too.

My interview lasted for about forty minutes and it was quite pleasant. Despite being a Hindi medium student, I did not face any problem during the interview. In the interview, I was asked many questions including the birthdays of great people. I was asked the name of the great man born on May 3. I started thinking. The interviewers asked me to think really hard. Finally, I replied that I was born on this day. Everyone laughed on hearing the answer. At that time, I felt that I was definitely selected in this exam. But I did not expect that I would get the 309th rank.

I would tell the students appearing for this exam that they should do what they are interested in. Parents should not impose their views on the children; rather they should help them set goals according to their interests. The movie '3 Idiots' is the best example in this case. In the movie, Aamir Khan topped the class because of his interest in that field. If Hindi medium students and poor students also set a goal of becoming an IAS officer based on their interest, then they can definitely be successful."

❑

9

IAS/IPS Exam: Preparing for the Interview

The interview is very important in any competitive exam. It is a part of oral communication. The people who conduct the interview are experienced, qualified and experts. Their job is to test the suitability of the candidates for a specific job. In an interview, they pay special attention to the following -

The personality of the candidate, his/her interest in the particular work, the sense of dedication and ability to understand the job, the level of his/her general knowledge and common sense, the aptitude and prudence from the point of view of the position of the competitor. The ability of the candidate is judged by assessing all the above-mentioned factors.

Personality

Personality is a combination of internal and external qualities of a person, such as - appearance of a person, presentation, style of conversation, method of question and answer, knowledge of the subject, method of expressing knowledge, character, enthusiasm, courage, and such moral qualities. Some parts of personality (such as shape and size) are God-given. But other qualities can be developed and grown. It is very important to strive for them because an impressive personality will help you win in the interview.

Interest and Dedication Towards Work

You should have a deep interest in the post for which you are a candidate. If it appears in the interview that you have minimal interest in that work or you are there due to some compulsion, then you may not be successful.

General Knowledge and Common Sense

Both of these elements help greatly in the interview. There is a difference between having common sense and knowing facts. If you have knowledge of facts, but do not have the sense to use them on the right occasion, then the knowledge obtained proves useless. Those questions can also be answered appropriately by common sense, about which you did not know before. This can be developed through study. If you have rich common sense, then you can prove very effective in the interview.

Position Wise Eligibility

You should try to develop those qualities that are proportionate to the position that you are a candidate for in yourself beforehand. For example, administrative posts, technical posts, judicial posts, managerial posts of economic institutions, etc. are posts of a specific nature. A different type of responsibility is associated with them. Some qualities are generally necessary for these posts, but the candidate should also have some special qualities, which you have to attempt to develop beforehand.

Some Important Things to Remember During the Interview

It is very important to remember some things during the interview process. If you do not conduct yourself according to these, then there can be adverse effects –

Do not enter the interview hall without permission.

Do not raise your hand while greeting.

You should sit on the chair in the interview room only after getting permission.

Be sure to say 'thank you' when you are asked to sit.

Do not interrupt the interviewers' conversation even if the subject of the conversation focuses on you.

Do not keep your briefcase, certificate files, etc. on the table in front of them.

It is not appropriate to enter or leave the room quickly. It is a sign of anxiety. Enter and exit with ease.

Do not attempt to speak unless you are asked a question.

Do not mock any person, organization, or political party in your answer.

Don't show your doubts or indecision in front of the interviewers.

If you do not know the answer to any question, then be honest about it. Do not state facts that you are uncertain about because the interviewers have full knowledge about them.

Do not speak exaggeratedly about yourself.

Do not present inconsistent arguments.

If you cough, sneeze, etc. during the interview, use a handkerchief.

Do not get into a religious debate, only talk about humanism.

If for some reason you do not understand the question, ask the interviewers to repeat the question by saying 'Pardon me please'. Do not answer the question without understanding it.

Make sure to use 'Shrimanji' or 'Sir/Madam' in conversation.

Do not use such words in the conversation that will display sycophancy.

Demonstrate courtesy and humility, never demonstrate arrogance and pride.

Don't be discouraged in the interview room. Don't let the feeling of indifference appear.

Answer the questions judiciously with a calm mind.

Truth-Formulating Habits

1. A dubious message can cause immense trouble. Therefore, before giving the message, prepare it well.
2. Whatever you say in conversation should be easily understood by other people. Otherwise, the message would be meaningless.
3. The message should be based on your experience and thoughts. Only then your confidence will reflect in it.
4. Writing is an art. It is important that you practise writing using technology to become proficient in it.
5. You should be firm in your thoughts in written communication. So, make sure that you prepare after looking at the previous record file.
6. Shakespeare said - "Brevity is the soul of wit." So, whatever you want to say or write, keep it brief. The concentration of mind is essential for this.
7. You should pay attention to two things in summary writing- (1) You should include the essential elements from the passage, (2) You should limit it to one-third words.

8. Solution and subscription are important in letter-writing. Their usage depends on whom you are writing the letter to.
9. In essay writing, the originality of your thoughts, imagination, subject-related knowledge level, and ability to explain are tested. So, choose the subject carefully.
10. You can use humour in your speech, but only if you have command over it.
11. Using appropriate body language while speaking doubly impacts the listeners. Therefore, you must know which gesture/sign should be used at the appropriate time.

Judge the person in front of you during the interview

If you propose to appear for the interview, the first requirement for your success is your educational qualification. But apart from this, there are some other things, which can be helpful for you to have a successful interview. One of these is pacing, that is, trying to act in the same way as the mood of the interviewer. This way you will be able to establish connections with them and your chances of success will increase. Generally, we like people who share a similar nature as ourselves. This is fully applicable in the case of a career as well.

You should sit in the interview in the same way as the interviewer is seated, provided it is a formal style of seating. You should try to maintain the same tone, voice, and words in the conversation as them in terms of your conduct. In practical life, these kinds of things can go a long way in helping you to adjust to other people.

You also have to be aware of the mood of the interviewer because they want the person sitting with them to share the same mood as them. It should not happen that the person in front is in a serious mood and you, on the other hand, display excessive enthusiasm. Your eagerness can make things difficult. If the environment is serious, then you should also answer in a serious manner. You just have to be aware of the way you are being spoken to. Experts call it 'pacing', i.e., you have to match the pace of the person in front. In other words, you can call it feeling another person's pulse.

In the Interview Room

Interview is the last and most important test in the civil service exam. Hence, it plays a major role in the final selection. Through the interview, the interview board virtually checks the entire personality of the candidate. The board members feel that the personality of the person who is going to be entrusted with such a huge responsibility should be perfect so that there would not be any problems in future.

Before appearing for the civil service interview, you should honestly assess your weaknesses such as nervousness, hasty attitude, over-enthusiasm and dishonesty and should avoid them. Although the interview board has the complete biodata of the candidate it asks questions related to it. That is why questions related to biodata should be prepared properly. The main exam is mostly sufficient for the knowledge of the subjects. Along with this, the questions from GS and GK are definitely asked, which have to be answered carefully.

After talking to the aspirants, it has been found that when the candidates face the interview board, they are nervous on the inside. Sometimes, candidates also start trembling due to nervousness. This condition exposes a weak personality and so, it should be avoided. In a panic mode, a person ends up saying what he should not and cannot say what he wants to. Sometimes, a candidate facing the board says meaningless things and he realizes that only when the chairman of the interview board asks them to leave or when he goes out and discusses the situation with his friends. That is why you should never panic.

Haste or over-enthusiasm is also risky during the interview.

Candidates tend to commit mistakes when they are over-enthusiastic and end up answering questions in a hurry. It is often seen that the candidate starts answering even before the board member has completed the question. This makes you look rude and brash. It is necessary for the interviewee to listen carefully to the question and answer it thoughtfully.

One should never try to lie in the interview. It has been observed that when the person taking the interview asks a question to the candidate and he does not know the answer, he tries to fool the interviewer by telling lies in different ways. This is wrong. Never try to fool the interviewers because they are much more senior and far ahead in knowledge and intelligence than you. Hence, they will look through your every move.

So, if you do not know the answer to a question, you should apologize and clearly decline to answer saying that you do not know the answer to the question. Often, when the candidate declines to answer a question, a member of the interview board answers it. You should listen to it carefully. In case you have any doubt about their answer, do not question them because they are not there to teach you but only to conduct your interview.

Tips for Success in the Interview

Hard work is the key to success. When you take up some work with passion and dedication, then the result is always commendable. Everyone wants to take up a job after studies, but only a few people get selected. By following some guidelines, we can be successful in any field. If you also want to crack the interview, then you can adopt some simple tips-

Be Punctual

Punctuality is very important in life. You should make it a habit to reach the venue a little earlier. This habit will help you in being successful. It is important to reach on time for the interview. In case you reach slightly before the appointed time, you can prepare yourself mentally by talking to other candidates, checking the interview panel and going through possible questions.

Pay Attention to Your Attire

You should pay special attention to your attire for the interview. You should wear neat and properly ironed clothes that are suitable for the occasion. Your hair should not be messy. Women should tie their long hair properly so that they do not have to adjust or tidy them repeatedly.

Be Well Prepared

Before going for the interview, you should learn details about the concerned post thoroughly. You should carry a copy of all your documents and certificates. At the time of the interview, you should hand over only the certificate which has been asked for and should not hand over any other certificate in a panic mode. You should not let your mind get distracted before the interview. You should think only about the possible questions so that when those questions are asked, you can answer them with full confidence and without any hesitation.

You should listen to the interviewer carefully – you should stay focused during the interview. You should listen carefully to each question so that you do not have to ask it to be repeated as doing so can dilute your impact. Frequently, people start answering the question with enthusiasm even before the question is completed. This has an adverse impression on the interview panel. So, you should answer with complete confidence. You should not be nervous. If you prepare well, you will definitely be successful.

Do Not Lie

Avoid a question that you do not know the answer to instead of pretending that you know a lot about the question. In such a situation, your chances of getting selected are minimal.

Your Body Language

Your body language should be calm during the interview. You should not move your hands or wipe your sweat repeatedly. A slight smile on the face will prove to be very effective.

Do Not Speak Loudly

During the interview, you should not answer in a loud voice or speak so softly that the interviewer cannot hear you. You should answer simply and in a pleasant voice. As far as possible, you should use measured words. You should give the interviewer a chance to speak too and not keep talking yourself.

Look at All the Panel Members

A variety of questions will come up when the interview panel consists of four or more members. It will be better if you answer politely by addressing everyone and include everyone in it.

Do Not Argue

You should not argue during the interview. Doing so will not prove your confidence or knowledge to the panel. You can convince the interviewer of your talent with confidence and humility and not by arguing. So, you should avoid an argument or dispute.

Weird or unusual Questions Asked During the IAS Interview

The Interview stage of the IAS Civil Services Exam is considered to be the toughest. Almost every candidate is nervous about this stage and there are reasons for it. Actually, there is no limit to the kind of questions at this stage, nor does it have any prescribed syllabus. It is also difficult to find the purpose of some questions. Many times, such questions come up during the interview that the candidates get confused.

The purpose of the IAS Civil Services Interview is not to assess the knowledge of the candidate. He has already appeared for the tests in two stages where his knowledge was assessed. The purpose of the interview is to test the presence of mind, attitude and thought process of the candidate.

That's why often interviewers ask such questions to the candidates whose purpose is to make them feel uncomfortable. Some such questions are given below. They seem somewhat strange, but their answers are not very difficult either.

- ***In which state is the Bay of Bengal?***
  Answer - Bay of Bengal is in liquid state.

- ***What would happen if a red coloured stone is thrown in the blue sea?***
  Answer - The stone will get wet and sink.

- ***Which animal lives in water but does not drink water?***
  Answer - Frog is an animal, which lives in water, but never drinks water.

- ***Which animal can hold its breath for 6 days?***
  Answer – Scorpion.

- ***What is it that only the one who owns it can see and can see only once?***
  Answer – A dream while sleeping.

- ***Name a thing which has the names of fruits, flowers and sweets together in it?***
  Answer – Gulab Jamun.

- ***Name a thing which breaks as soon as it is mentioned.***
  Answer – Silence.

- ***How do you get the answer '1' if 2 is added to 11?***
  Answer - When the clock strikes 11, adding 2 to it makes it 1.

- ***Who owns the Internet?***
  Answer - The owner of the Internet is the one who gets it installed.

- ***Which animal can never jump?***
  Answer - Elephant. As an elephant is a very big and heavy animal, it can never jump.

- ***What will happen if the amount of oxygen on earth gets doubled?***
  Answer - If the amount of oxygen in our atmosphere gets doubled, then the size of small insects, cockroaches, etc. will become huge. This would be exactly as shown in Hollywood movies sometimes.

- ***Which part of the human body keeps changing every two months?***
  Answer - Eyebrows.

- ***Why do we drink water?***
  Answer - Because we cannot eat and chew water.

- ***What is the difference between search and research?***
  Answer - Research means making new discoveries, while search means finding answers to questions that already exist.

- ***Which flower weighs 10 kg?***
  Answer – Rafflesia. It is found in Indonesia and Malaysia. It weighs up to 10 kg.

- ***A man is sitting in a dark room where there is no lantern, mobile or light. So, how is he reading?***
  Answer - The person sitting in the room is blind. He is reading with the help of Braille script, for which light is not required.

These are just some instances mentioned here as examples so that when you prepared for the interview, you would remember that you can be asked any kind of question and your personality is being checked through the question that is being asked.

Success Story: Elevate yourself so much...

2012 batch IAS topper S. Divyadarshini says, "There is no substitute for hard work. If you want to crack the IAS exam, you have to be passionate and hardworking. Only those students who have these qualities can crack this exam." Divyadharshini, a law graduate from Dr. Ambedkar Law University, Tamil Nadu, says she had chosen public administration and law. She prepared both subjects with planning and she kept rectifying her shortcomings. Along with her family members, her mentor Prabhakaran Sir played an important role in her success. They supported Divyadharshini a lot.

Her mother is a housewife and her father is a customs consultant. She started her preparations immediately after graduation. She was interviewed at the Rajni Razdan board, which went very well. She hoped to get selected after the exam, but she did not really hope that she would be a topper. She says, "I would like to say to the students preparing for this exam that if you believe yourself to be capable, then you will be automatically successful. Do not be afraid if you fail, but try twice as hard because you may achieve your goal in the last attempt."

❑

10

On the Edge of the Destination

If your dream is to become an administrative officer, then getting IAS/IPS training is considered the first step towards realizing your dream. This training is often described as lively, exciting, and satisfying. During training, officers develop a deep sense of achievement and self-development. Knowing about the kind of training that IAS/IPS officers receive will definitely add excitement to your preparation.

After clearing all three stages of the IAS/IPS exam, every candidate is taken to the Lal Bahadur Shastri National Academy of Administration (LBSNAA) where they are given training by senior training officers.

Phase I of IAS Training

In the first phase, officer trainees of the Indian Administrative Services are given rigorous training in various subjects to enable them to handle a wide range of tasks they would handle in their first decade of service. It consists of district training. However, before that, come the following two modules -

1. Winter Study Tour

The probationers travel across the country to experience its rich cultural diversity, also known as *Bharat Darshan*. A week's training with the Bureau of Parliamentary Studies exposes them to the working of the parliamentary system in India. At this stage the officer trainees are also introduced to the President of India, the Vice President, the Prime Minister and other important dignitaries.

2. Academic Module

It is a theme-based module and covers a wide variety of topics such as Policy Formulation, National Security/Law and Order, Agriculture/Land Management and Administration, Rural Development/Decentralization and Panchayati Raj, Urban Management/Infrastructure and Public-Private Partnership, E-Governance/Office Administration/IAS Approach/Role in Administration. In this phase, soft skills (leadership, organizational behaviour and interpersonal skills), project management, engineering skills and skills such as ICIT financial management and project appraisal, social sector/weaker sections and minorities are given special attention.

IAS Probationers are given one year of district training which is like a drill to enable them to see, understand and live the quintessential India with its amazing diversities, myriad challenges and opportunities. It provides them with diverse opportunities to understand the administrative set-up. It also gives them an opportunity to interact with the people, their representatives and officials to understand the development paradigm as well as the effectiveness of the strategies.

Phase II of IAS Training

In the second phase, the officer trainees are given a platform to share their respective experiences in the field and are enabled to understand the strengths and weaknesses of the administration and governance of the country. In this phase, the emphasis is on interactive teaching methodology. There are also special sessions by eminent experts working in the government and outside the government. In the phase before the end of the training, the officer trainees prepare for their career in government service. The penultimate phase of training provides a vibrant learning opportunity to officer trainees before they embark on a career in government service.

IAS officers under training are encouraged to lead a rich, diverse, and vibrant campus life beyond the confines of the lecture hall. Some examples of such experiences are as follows –

Trainees are sent for trekking in the Greater Himalayas, where they learn to live in adverse conditions, inclement weather, inadequate accommodation and limited food. Visits and stay in backward villages to understand the realities of rural life are an integral part of the entry-level programme. Officer trainees are encouraged to join extra-curricular modules and gain proficiency in any hobby of their choice. For that, they are encouraged to participate in creative activities of various clubs and societies to express their creative potential.

IPS Training

Nowadays, there is an increasing craze for becoming an IPS officer among the youth. Hence, many questions keep arising in their minds regarding the IPS training. For example, where the training takes place, what they learn in training, how long the training lasts etc. These are some of the questions which often occur to those who dream of becoming an IPS officer.

IPS training is considered to be the toughest training in our country as IPS officers have to command the Armed Police Force in all the Indian States and Union Territories of the country. Learning about the training imparted to IPS officers not only infuses a new fervour among the aspirants but also gives them a strong motivation to prepare. The training of IPS is also done in sandwich format just like IAS – here sandwich means, the format of training is like a sandwich - first in the academy, then in the field and then again in the academy.

Lal Bahadur Shastri National Academy of Administration (LBSNAA) Phase I (Foundation Course)

The Academy not only works for civil service capacity building but also focuses on inter-service camaraderie and cooperation. The objective of the Foundation Course is to establish familiarity and coordination between the newly recruited officers of All India Services and Central Services (Group 'A'). It teaches new officers the required skills, knowledge and conduct.

The main objectives of the Foundation Course are to establish greater cooperation and coordination among various public services and to encourage an all-round development of an officer trainee's personality, which may be a combination of intellectual, moral and physical development.

After the foundation course, IPS trainees are sent to the Sardar Vallabhbhai Patel National Police Academy in Hyderabad, where their training process is completed.

The Sardar Vallabhbhai Patel National Police Academy (SVPNPA) has been entrusted with the task of transforming young IPS officer trainees into professional police officers. The Sardar Vallabhbhai Patel National Police Academy, Hyderabad, is the premier institution for the training of Indian Police Service (IPS) officers.

There are two phases in the second phase of IPS training. The first phase begins at the National Police Academy in Hyderabad. IPS officers also undergo training in a district of their cadre for a fixed period of time between two phases of training at the IPS Academy.

IPS trainees join the Sardar Vallabhbhai Patel National Police Academy, Hyderabad for the second phase of training, which is called the Basic Training Course. This phase is of 11 months duration where the IPS officer trainees study various indoor, outdoor and aptitude subjects.

Basic Training

The objective of basic training is to build the capability of the officer trainees to be able to meet the challenges of police duty. The aim of the training is to ensure that the officers acquire the necessary skills, knowledge, understanding, attitudes and practices to effectively discharge the duties of a police officer. This training enables officer trainees to undertake initial assignments and subsequently various senior supervisory assignments up to the rank of Superintendent of Police in District and Special Units of the Police Department.

The 'Integrated Training' model used in the Academy for imparting training focuses on the integration of three dimensions - Sensitization (personal and social), Guidance (ethical and legal) and Competence (domain and inter-departmental). The National Police Academy inculcates human values in IPS trainees, which help them not only to be competent police officers but also to be effective and well-rounded human beings.

The second phase helps in increasing the knowledge about the allotted state cadre, which includes the language, traditions, culture, etc. This training takes place in the State Police Academies and is of three weeks duration. This phase also includes a component of practical training, where the trainees are given the responsibility of handling legal matters in police stations. IPS trainees are also attached to Police Headquarters, where they are exposed to district level proceedings. This phase is of six months duration.

During their training at the Sardar Vallabhbhai Patel National Police Academy, officer trainees are 'attached' to various units of the Army-Air Force, Navy, and Central Armed Police Forces (CRPF), which helps them appreciate the role of other organizations in nation building. The passing out parade of officer trainees is held after 11 months.

Lal Bahadur Shastri National Academy of Administration (LBSNAA)'s Bharat Darshan Yatra

Every IAS aspirant is well aware of the Lal Bahadur Shastri National Academy of Administration. This is the first stop to their destination.

Every IAS aspirant looks forward to Bharat Darshan during the training phase at LBSNAA, Mussoorie. It is an experience that IAS trainees eagerly look forward to. Bharat Darshan is also called 'Winter Study Tour' and it is of eight weeks' duration. During this period, the officer trainees travel all over India to know as much as possible about the country and get a glimpse of the problems faced by people. It is an eye-opening experience for them.

Bharat Darshan begins during the first week of December, when snowfall starts in Mussoorie. This is one of the most interesting parts of training. The tour lasts for eight weeks and during this time the IAS trainees travel almost all over the country. Trainees who are appointed to other services such as IPS, IFS, etc. do not get such extensive travel opportunities. Of course, they do travel during their training to other institutes as well, but perhaps none is as extensive as the Bharat Darshan for IAS officers.

Generally, trainees are divided into groups of 9 – 10 members and a team leader is appointed for each team. Each team is sent to different places and all return to Mussoorie at the same time at the end of the Bharat Darshan. Usually, Bharat Darshan starts in the month of December and continues till the end of February.

This special training tour enables the trainees to know about the ecological, historical and cultural background prevalent in different regions of India. Trainees get an opportunity to know various institutions of national importance like RBI, SEBI, NGOs and their functioning in the nation building. For this purpose, Bharat Darshan has different attachments. These various attachments help to imbibe the soul of India and its pursuits. Some of the attachments are as follows - Army Attachment, IAF Attachment, Navy Attachment, NGO Attachment, Public Sector Attachment, Forest and Island Attachment.

The purpose of the visit is written in the course booklet of LBSNAA. It says, "to expose officer trainees to a wide range of organizations and situations during their careers and to give them a glimpse of the diversity of our cultural heritage."

Here, they get a first-hand account and experience of the work done by various institutions. This enables them to understand the problems and difficulties faced by the public and the authorities and people trying to help them. During this, the trainees get to experience various situations. On one hand they get the opportunity to stay in big hotels, on the other hand, they have to sleep on the floor in simple huts.

They meet eminent personalities, who talk to them about their work. All these trainees are able to understand and appreciate the diversity in India as they travel across the country, even facing life-threatening situations in Kashmir and other troubled areas of the country. Most of the IAS officers remember this experience as a life-changing and humbling journey.

What happens in the training at Sardar Vallabhbhai Patel National Police Academy?

The Indian Police Service is a very prestigious service of the IAS. Every year lakhs of people try to enter this service, but only a select few are successful. How difficult it is to work in the police can be gauged from the training given before the appointment in the service.

An IPS officer trainee is given training in 4 parts. The first is a 3-month foundation course at LBSNAA, Mussoorie, in which basic knowledge is imparted. After that, they have to go to Hyderabad. There they receive 11 months' training at the Sardar Vallabhbhai Patel National Police Academy. IPS officers are given district practical training for 6 months. The training of an IPS officer takes place first in the academy, then in the field and then again in the academy.

Compulsory indoor subjects for IPS consists of physical fitness which includes PT, athletics, gym, sports, cross country run up to 20 kms. All this is part of the training of an IPS officer. Officer trainees are also taught drill, yoga, unarmed combat and swimming during their training. This training is given to all IPS officers so that they are prepared to deal with any adverse situation.

Apart from this, the IPS officer is also given training in field craft, map reading, and ambush seating. During training, they are also taught how to easily foil any move of the enemy. Trainees are also given rock climbing training, assault training and weapon training in which assembling/disassembling, firing of revolver, pistol, machine gun, rifle, mortar, grenade are taught. Simply put, an IPS officer is given training in almost all weapons.

During their training at the Sardar Vallabhbhai Patel National Police Academy, officer trainees are 'attached' to various units of the Army, Air Force, Navy, and Central Armed Police Forces (CRPF), which helps them to understand the role of other organizations in nation building.

Responsibilities/Duties of IAS

The life of an IAS officer is very inspiring and difficult. You may have often heard stories of IAS officers who brought about a major change in a particular place with their work. In fact, the civil servants have played a key role in taking our country to where it is today. That's why Sardar Patel called them the 'steel frame' of Indian governance.

IAS officers have the potential to bring about a positive change in society - a change that society needs in order to develop. Keeping in mind the important position of an IAS officer, it would be fair to say that the role of an IAS officer is challenging as well as satisfying and at times even exciting.

Functions of an IAS Officer

The main functions of an IAS officer are as follows –

Management of government affairs including policy formulation, implementation and feedback.

Consulting various departments and elected representatives and taking collective steps towards development.

To manage the allocated public funds for better implementation of various schemes.

Monitoring the implementation of various government schemes and policies.

Responding to and coordinating relief operations in response to emergencies such as natural calamities, major accidents and riots. For example, during Covid-19, the responsibilities of an IAS officer increased manifold.

Apart from the above, there are three types of roles and responsibilities of an IAS officer.

Field Assessment

This is considered to be the most difficult and challenging task for an IAS officer. The first job of an IAS officer after training is usually a field job.

Responsibility at Sub-Divisional Level

As a Sub-Divisional Officer, the responsibilities of an IAS officer mainly include maintenance of law and order, development and administrative management.

Responsibility at the District Level

As a District Magistrate, Collector or Deputy Commissioner, an IAS officer performs the same functions as the SDM and this includes overseeing all the functions of the SDM.

State Secretariat/Public Sector Undertakings

After field posting, IAS officers are usually posted in the State Secretariat. Their first-hand experience helps them advise the elected representatives regarding making policies and taking decisions on government procedures. Also, many officers are posted on deputation to the PSU cadres and become part of the top management of various PSUs such as power discoms, industrial units, etc.

Central Secretariat

After the state secretariat, IAS officers usually get the secretary-level positions in various ministries at the central government level. Officers at this level are usually concerned with policy review, formulation and implementation.

Powers of IAS Officer

Code of Criminal Procedure (1973): Sections 107, 108, 109, 110, 133, 144, and 176 list the powers given to magistrates to maintain law and order.

The tenancy laws specify the revenue powers of a collector.

The National Disaster Management Act lists the powers of chief secretaries and district magistrates (magistrates) in directing operations for disaster relief. This act was widely used during the Covid-19 pandemic.

The Arms Act, Drug License Act, Essential Commodities Act, etc. list the powers of IAS officers to enforce regulations in critical situations.

However, one should not think that these powers are unrestricted. Officers can exercise their powers under these laws, but they are bound by the IAS rules and regulations. Therefore, they are answerable to the state and central government legislatures for their actions.

Responsibilities/Duties of IPS

The internal security of our country is completely in the hands of the policemen and the command of these policemen is in the hands of an IPS officer. So it can also be said that the responsibility of an IPS officer is tremendous and to fulfil them, they need courage as well as common sense.

An IPS officer's position is only a post, which gives powers to the personnel of State Police and all Indian Central Armed Police Forces. But with great positions come great responsibilities. The IPS officer of every district is the head of police officers, Superintendent of Police (SP) and Deputy Commissioner of Police (DSP). Apart from this, it is also part of the duties and responsibilities of an IPS officer to sort out any glitches or hurdles in the police machinery of the area.

The main task of the officers selected in the Indian Police Service is to maintain law and order. IPS officers do the job of implementing the law properly in the country. For this, IPS officers have to go through rigorous training. The primary duty of the IPS is to ensure that the people in their jurisdiction remain safe and that all officers in the district work to maintain law and order.

The most important responsibilities of an IPS officer are as follows -

- Prevention of crime
- Preventing accidents (socio-economic, etc.)
- Disaster Management
- Crime Investigation
- Registration for First Information Report (FIR)
- Granting permission for political/religious functions

Apart from heading the state police, an IPS officer also heads central police organizations like the National Security Guard, Intelligence Bureau, CBI, BSF, Indo-Tibetan Border Police and CRPF. Here, they play the role of commander. These officers head the police forces of the states and union territories. They also have to work with the Indian Army for some time in case of deployment of army in the area for special purposes.

IPS officers in the State Police play a pivotal role in maintaining peace in the allotted district. They are an integral part of all law-and-order decisions in the district that are involved in peacekeeping operations carried out inside the city. In addition, they have to ensure that there is no physical or economic damage to property or people in their allotted area. They are also responsible for the security of VIPs. In particular, they are responsible for the protection of the Chief Ministers and the Prime Minister.

Disaster and crisis management is also the responsibility of an IPS officer, such as identifying the causes of disaster and effectively managing crisis situations to protect people. For example - in case of riots or disaster, the IPS officer can call an immediate meeting of the armed forces or NDRF to maintain order in the situation of lawlessness.

The police force is a department through which one can really make a difference in the society at all levels. But in India, working conditions for the police are far from ideal. The technologies have become obsolete and often our IPS officers have to work in the same old conditions. Not only this, the IPS has to work within the framework of the legal system, which in itself is very restrictive and slow.

The IAS is a public social service, while the IPS is a mandatory service to maintain law and order. There are many unique opportunities to do social service while working in the IPS, which an IAS officer may never get. There is no limit to the responsibilities of a police officer. From organizing traffic duties to managing the rules and regulations to protect the life and property of citizens are also their duties.

Salary of an IAS Officer

The Civil Services Examination is the dream of many youths of the country. Lakhs of people work hard to pass it, but only a few people are successful. The Civil Services Examination accepts applications for appointment to about 24 services and all these services are awarded on the basis of different priorities and ranks. Now it is obvious that when the services are different, their scope and remuneration will also be different.

Now we know that most of the candidates want to become IAS officers in the civil services and we also know that to become an IAS officer, one has to get a top rank. As can be seen from the ranking itself, the post of an IAS officer is higher and hence their salary is also higher as compared to other services.

As per the Seventh Pay Commission, the basic pay of any IAS officer is Rs. 56,100. Apart from this, IAS officers also get many other allowances, including travelling allowance and dearness allowance. According to reports, after adding all allowances, an IAS officer gets a total salary of more than Rs 1 lakh per month in the initial days. The salary of an IAS officer is governed by the grade of IAS officers. Grades are given to IAS officers based on the number of years in service. The grades of IAS officers are regularly upgraded on the basis of their experience. Sometimes they are also promoted on the basis of their performance. Their salary structure is divided into 8 grades. Each grade has a fixed basic pay and grade pay.

Various Posts and Basic Salary

Name of the Post	Years of Service	Basic Pay
SDM Under Secretary Assistant Secretary	1-4 years	₹56100
ADM Deputy Secretary Under Secretary	5-8 years	₹67700

District Magistrate Joint Secretary Deputy Secretary	9-12 years	₹78800
District Magistrate Deputy Secretary Director	13-16 years	₹118500
Divisional Commissioner Secretary-cum-Commissioner		
Joint Secretary	16-24 years	₹144200
Divisional Commissioner Principal Secretary Additional Secretary	25-30 years	₹182200
Additional Chief Secretary	30-33 years	₹205400
Chief Secretary and Secretary	34-36 years	₹225000
Cabinet Secretary	More than 37 years	₹250000

Similarly, according to the Seventh Pay Commission, an IPS officer gets a salary of ₹56,100. Apart from the basic salary, the IPS officer also gets dearness allowance and many other types of allowances. An IPS officer can reach the post of DGP after promotion and the officer in the post of DGP gets the highest salary. The salary structure of the IPS is as follows–

DSP	They get a salary of 56 thousand 100 rupees.
ASP	They get a salary of 67 thousand 700 rupees.
SP	After reaching this post, the IPS officer gets a salary of 78 thousand 800 rupees.
SSP	The salary of officers in this post is Rs 1 lakh 18 thousand 500.
DIG	This IPS officer gets a salary of Rs 1 lakh 31 thousand 100.
IG	They get a monthly salary of ₹1 lakh 44 thousand 200.
ADGP	On reaching this rank, IPS officers get a salary of ₹ 2 lakh 5 thousand 400.

DGP	This is the highest post among IPS officers. The officer in this post gets the highest salary. His monthly salary is Rs 2 lakh 25 thousand.

According to the Seventh Pay Commission, now every IRS officer gets a salary according to his basic pay and TA, DA, HRA.

Salary Structure of IRS Officers

Designation	**Pay Scale**
Assistant Commissioner of Income Tax	15,600 - 39100 + 1400 grade salary
Deputy Commissioner of Income Tax	15,600 - 39100 + 6600 grade salary
Joint Commissioner of Income Tax	15,600 - 39100 + 7600 grade salary
Additional Commissioner of Income Tax	37,400 - 67,000 + 8700 grade salary
Commissioner of Income Tax	37,400 - 67,000 + 10000 grade salary
Principal Commissioner of Income Tax	75,000 to 80,000
Chief Commissioner of Income Tax	75,000 to 80,000
Principal Chief Commissioner of Income Tax	80,000 Fixed

Apart from the basic pay and perks, an IRS officer gets many other perks such as medical facility, electricity and water bills, options for studying abroad, free phone calls, pension and retirement benefits, security guards and domestic help, apartment (2 or 3 BHK) and transportation.

How to Become a Successful IAS/IPS Officer

Every aspirant preparing for the IAS/IPS works hard and invests both his energy and time. During preparation, he not only adds to his knowledge, but also develops some qualities. These qualities and habits stay with him not only during his preparation but even after he becomes an IAS officer and come in handy in his professional life as well.

The biggest quality of successful IAS/IPS aspirants is that they work hard all the time to achieve one goal after another. Even after they become IAS/IPS officers, they do not sit idly but continue planning to be more successful in future. In fact, this quality develops inside a person as a result of his habits. Therefore, if you also want to become a successful IAS/IPS officer, then you should also develop these habits.

Evaluate Yourself

You must keep evaluating yourself at regular intervals. Take out enough time to test yourself through practice and mock tests on a daily, weekly or monthly basis. By doing your own evaluation, you will not only be able to find your mistakes, but gradually your mistakes will also start reducing. Apart from this, evaluate yourself also compared to others, especially those whom you consider better than yourself.

Focus on Here and Now

You should focus on the present leaving the failures of the past behind. Instead of getting discouraged by thinking about past failures, one should try to improve the future. If you make such efforts consistently, it will definitely become a source of inspiration for you and result in not only a pleasant IAS/IPS preparation but also an agreeable professional life thereafter.

Learn from Failures

Everyone experiences failure. But someone who does not move forward even after facing failure will not be successful in the future either. On the other hand, the chances of someone being successful who moves forward without thinking about that failure are also negligible. If you failed, you should ask yourself what mistakes you committed and why those mistakes happened Find the answers to these questions and move ahead resolving firmly in your mind that those mistakes will not occur again.

Take charge of situations

Many people work under the IAS/IPS officer, who wait for his orders in every other situation. An efficient IAS/IPS officer is expected to guide his/her subordinates properly. As an IAS/IPS aspirant, if you feel that you cannot develop leadership qualities within yourself, then believe me, it would be very difficult for you to become an IAS/IPS officer. This is the first quality that people on the interview panel who ask questions look for in any candidate. They test it with their questions and your thoughts about different situations. To develop this quality, first develop your own thoughts and start presenting them articulately.

Positivity

It is essential to be positive in life. It is a quality that gives you the courage to face the biggest obstacles. To become a successful IAS/IPS officer, you need to imbibe this quality. An IAS/IPS officer cannot feel helpless in any situation. We saw a concrete example of this during the Corona pandemic, when the general public in our country did not face any major problem even during the lockdown. Be it provision of free rations to the poor or delivery of essential commodities to the needy, various administrative officers of our country ensured all this took place efficiently.

❑❑❑